INSIDE THE AN

Penelop
Poppaea

· ———— ·

Women in Greek and Roman Society

INSIDE THE ANCIENT WORLD

General Editor: M. R. F. Gunningham

Other titles in the series

Robin Barrow: *Athenian Democracy*
Robin Barrow: *Greek and Roman Education*
Jenny Gibbon: *Athenian Society*
Anne Haward: *Penelope to Poppaea*
Massey and Moreland: *Slavery in Ancient Rome*
David Taylor: *Cicero and Rome*
R. D. Williams: *Aeneas and the Roman Hero*
David Taylor: *Roman Society*

By the same author

Sparta
Plato, Utilitarianism and Education
Moral Philosophy for Education

with R. G. Woods
Introduction to Philosophy of Education

INSIDE THE ANCIENT WORLD

PENELOPE TO POPPAEA

Women in Greek and Roman Society

ANNE HAWARD

Nelson

Thomas Nelson and Sons Ltd
Nelson House   Mayfield Road
Walton-on-Thames   Surrey
KT12 5PL   UK

51 York Place
Edinburgh
EH1 3JD   UK

Thomas Nelson (Hong Kong) Ltd
Toppan Building 10/F
22A Westlands Road
Quarry Bay   Hong Kong

Thomas Nelson Australia
102 Dodds Street
South Melbourne
Victoria 3205   Australia

Nelson Canada
1120 Birchmount Road
Scarborough Ontario
M1K 5G4   Canada

First published by Macmillan Education Ltd 1990
ISBN 0-333-47604-2

This edition published by Thomas Nelson and Sons Ltd 1992

ISBN 0-17-438513-7
NPN 9 8 7 6 5 4 3

Printed in Hong Kong.

Contents

Illustrations   vi

Acknowledgements   vii

Introduction   1

1 The world of Homer   3

2 The Archaic Age   11

3 Women in Classical Athens   17

4 Leading ladies – women in Greek drama   28

5 The Roman *matrona* – the early Republican ideal   38

6 The Late Republic – a changing scene   56

7 Imperial laws and Imperial ladies   68

8 Contrasts – working women and ladies of leisure   79

Conclusion   88

Index   90

Illustrations

1 The goddesses Athene and Hera   5
2 Circe leaves her loom to give Odysseus a magic potion   7
3 Women weaving and weighing wool   8–9
4 Woman following plough-ox to sow seed   12
5 Spartan girl athlete   15
6 Marriage procession: taking a bride to her new home   20
7 Women at home admiring a necklace   21
8 Women fetching water from the fountain house   24
9 *Hetairai* entertaining at a drinking party   25
10 Girls in the Panathenaic procession   26
11 Woman with offerings at a tomb   29
12 Sacrifice of Polyxena   31
13 Electra and Orestes murder Aegisthus   33
14 Vestal Virgin   44
15 Childbirth   47
16 Mother nursing baby while father looks on   48
17 *Dextrarum iunctio*: a couple join hands in marriage   52
18 Tombstone of Avita   60
19 A literary lady   62
20 Living the life of a prostitute   66
21 Livia, wife of Augustus   74
22 Poppaea, wife of Nero   77
23 Four maids to attend the mistress's hairstyle   80
24 Woman bookkeeper in a butcher's shop   82
25 Statue of Eumachia put up in Pompeii   86
   Cover   Athenian woman pouring a libation to the gods

Acknowledgements

The author and publishers wish to acknowledge, with thanks, the following photographic sources: Ashmoleum Museum, Oxford, pages 21, 29; Trustees of the British Museum, pages 24, 31, 52, 60, 77; Landesmuseum, Trier, page 80; Lauros – Giraudon, page 66; Mansell Collection, pages 7, 12, 25, 33, 44, 47, 48, 82, 86; National Museums and Galleries on Merseyside, page 15; New York Metropolitan Museum of Art, 07.286.36, Rogers Fund 1907, page 5; New York Metropolitan Museum of Art, 31.11.10, Fletchers Fund 1931, pages 8/9; Sheridan Photo Library, pages 15, 20, 26; Werner Forman Archives, page 62.

The publishers have made every effort to trace the copyright holders, but if they have inadvertently overlooked any, they will be pleased to make the necessary arrangements at the first opportunity.

Introduction

What was life like for a woman in the ancient world? Were all Greek women devoted faithful wives like Penelope or vengeful murderers like Clytemnestra? Did Roman women spend their time like Poppaea in the extravagant orgies that film-makers show us?

Before trying to distinguish fact from fiction, we must consider how we get our information. The literary evidence concerning women was all written by men, but not in order to tell us how women lived. They were writing for some other purpose: to prove a court case; to win the prize for tragedy, by stirring an audience, or for comedy, with an outrageous plot; to expound a theory; or to record historical events. To fill out the picture we can also look at archaeological evidence of how people lived and worshipped, at inscriptions, laws, and scenes from vases and reliefs.

The evidence of art

The illustrations in art books can be studied for the information they provide as well as appreciated as works of art. Most public sculpture concerned men or gods and goddesses, but the purpose of the *korai* statues of beautiful young girls in their best clothes is not agreed; they may have been dedicated as ideals or to commemorate an individual girl's service to the goddess. This also seems to be the purpose of the figures of children with animals found in Artemis' sanctuary at Brauron. A small figurine of a girl runner in a short tunic seems to represent a Spartan girl. There are also grave *stelai* with detailed reliefs showing women bidding farewell to their sorrowing families, or with a maid or baby.

Black-figure vases, and the later red-figure vases, illustrate much of the daily life of women in Archaic and Classical Athens and are worth careful study. In black-figure scenes one can see the elaborate clothes of the period which women spent so much of

1

their time producing, and details of dress, hairstyles, caps and furniture are clearly shown – the crowned bride in her marriage procession, the bride and groom going off in a chariot, the callers with wedding presents, women fetching water, women bathing, weaving, spinning. These vases were in daily use and it is fair to assume that they illustrate what men expected of women.

Books on Roman art also can help to build up our picture of women's life. The relief sculptures from Roman shop signs, funeral monuments and friezes show scenes from everyday life. There are also many portrait busts, ranging from the sensible wives and mothers of the Republic to the court beauties with elaborate hairstyles of the Empire. The study of wall-paintings needs care; many are imaginative compositions based on Greek myths, but there are some that do represent real life, such as the portraits of the baker and his wife or the girl being dressed for her wedding that were found in Pompeii.

It is interesting to compare the life of women in the ancient world with our own experience, but misleading to introduce present-day concerns and attitudes into our interpretation.

1

The World of Homer

Minoans and Myceneans

Our knowledge of these earliest Greek societies comes chiefly from archaeology.

Excavations at the large Minoan palace-complexes in Crete and Santorini have unearthed many female figurines and frescos. Some show goddesses and priestesses, and seem to indicate the worship of a mother goddess. Others show palace ladies in sophisticated dress. From exquisite jewellery and figurines of ladies dancing it appears that wealthy women enjoyed considerable respect and social freedom then, but there is no written evidence about their life or the life of the poorer women.

In the Mycenean society that followed in the late Bronze Age, palace records were written on baked clay tablets in Linear B script. The tablets found at Pylos give the tasks performed by women as fetching water, giving baths, spinning, weaving and grinding corn – and all on less than half the food men received! It seems that by this time there was a clear distinction between the roles of men and women.

Goddesses and women in mythology

The earliest ideas about women are found not in history but in mythology. These stories of gods and heroes show how men tried to explain the world they lived in. Later, in about 700 BC, they were organised by Hesiod into a poem called 'Theogony'. This tells how Ge (Mother Earth), with her children, overthrew the god Uranus, and how Cronus in turn was overthrown by *his* wife and children. Zeus thus became the king of gods and men and no longer allowed women to have such power. Some scholars argue from these myths that originally there was matriarchy (rule by women), but there is no conclusive evidence for this, even in societies that worshipped a mother goddess.

In the *Iliad* and the *Odyssey*, Homer makes it clear that the goddesses surrounding Zeus are all firmly under his power and can be called to order on Mount Olympus like naughty children. When Aphrodite is wounded in battle trying to help her son, Aeneas, Zeus makes her role clear:

The father of gods and men smiled and calling golden Aphrodite, he said: 'My child, deeds of war are not for you. You attend to love and marriage. Swift Ares and Athene will look after all this warfare.'

[Homer, *Iliad* V 426–30]

Aphrodite, 'the weaver of plots', possessed 'love and desire by which both men and gods can be overpowered'. This power of women to make men act irrationally may have been one of the reasons for men's distrust of them.

Each goddess seems to represent a different part of men's experience of women. Hera, although the powerful patroness of marriage and women, is a jealous wife and constantly quarrels with Zeus, as he tells Thetis when she asks for help:

Then greatly troubled Zeus the cloud-gatherer said: 'This is disastrous. You will make me quarrel with Hera, when she infuriates me with reproaches. She always scolds me in front of the other immortal gods and says I help the Trojans in battle. But you go away again now, in case Hera notices anything. I will look after everything and settle it.'...

So then Zeus sat down on his throne; Hera looked at him and knew that silver-footed Thetis, daughter of the old man of the sea, had been making plans with him. She immediately addressed Zeus, son of Cronus, mockingly: 'Who's been making plans with you, crafty one? You always like to steer clear of me and reach your decisions secretly. You can never bear to confide in me.'

[Homer, *Iliad* I 517–23, 536–43]

Artemis was seen as a cool, detached goddess, a virgin and the protector of animals. She was also concerned with the physical side of women's life, pregnancy and childbirth, perhaps because of her connection with the monthly cycle of the moon. A woman who died unexpectedly was said to have been slain by Artemis.

The most complex goddess is Athene, who was born from the head of Zeus and so shared her father's wisdom, which was normally a male attribute. She was a virgin warrior, normally represented in armour, yet she was patron of all the female arts of spinning and weaving. Of all the gods she was the readiest to help mortals by deflecting a weapon in battle or wrapping them in a useful protective mist. She appeared in disguise to give advice, or came to the rescue as when Poseidon wrecked Odysseus' raft:

But Athene, daughter of Zeus, thought otherwise. She checked the course of the other winds and bade them all die down and sleep, but she roused a rushing North Wind and broke down the waves before him, so that Odysseus, descendent of Zeus, might escape death and fate and come among the seafaring Phaeacians.   [Homer, *Odyssey* V 382–7]

Two main types of mortal women figure in mythology: those who became the mistresses of gods, and those of manlike strength of character who committed outrageous deeds. The stories of women like Alcmene and Semele show beautiful women as the playthings of the gods, the gods caring more about the children they beget than about the fate of the women themselves. Some of these stories may have been invented to provide a family with an impressive ancestry, but they show how men thought of women. Stories like those of Medea killing her own sons, Scylla betraying her father, Hecabe blinding Polymnestor, or Clytemnestra murdering her husband, seem to show a deep distrust of women as violent and unpredictable beings (a view which is further illustrated in Chapter 5):

Thus the ghost of Agamemnon spoke, but I [Odysseus] said in answer, 'Alas, truly far-thundering Zeus has borne terrible hatred for the House of

The goddesses Athene and Hera

5

Atreus from the beginning through the wiles of women. For Helen's sake many of us perished, but for you Clytemnestra devised her trap while you were far away.' So I spoke, but he at once replied, 'Now you too be sure never to be too soft to your wife and don't reveal all the counsel you know, but tell part and keep the rest secret. But death will not come to you, Odysseus, from your wife, for very prudent and intelligent is the daughter of Icarios, the wise Penelope. ... But my wife did not let me satisfy my eyes with the sight of my son. Before that she murdered me, her husband. But I will tell you another thing and do you take it to heart. Bring your ship to your dear homeland in secret, not openly, for no longer is there any trust in women.'   [Homer, *Odyssey* XI 435–57]

Women in Homer

Homer's poems provide the first accounts of women's life. The traditional date of the fall of Troy is 1184 BC, but Homer's poems were passed orally from bard to bard and were not written down until the sixth century BC, so the details of everyday life so vividly described cannot be pinned to an exact date.

The bards who told these tales after banquets in the hall of the local chief were teaching as well as entertaining. Hearing of Hector or Odysseus, men learnt to be clever, resourceful and brave in war. What models were presented for women?

'Go into the house and get on with your own work, weaving and spinning, and tell your slave-girls to perform their tasks. Talking is men's concern.'   [Homer, *Odyssey* I 356–9 and *Iliad* VI 490–2]

These words are used twice by Telemachus to his mother, Penelope, when he asserts his position as lord of the *oikos* (household) in the absence of Odysseus. They are also used by Hector to his wife, Andromache, when she has been watching the battle from the walls of Troy and has spotted a vulnerable place. Hector, however, sends her indoors as 'war is man's concern'.

Greeks and Trojans alike claimed that they were fighting for their wives and children. Everyone knew the fate of the defeated when their menfolk had been killed. Hector, who is a loving husband, says:

'The fate of Troy does not move me as much as your grief when some bronze-clad Achaean leads you away weeping and robs you of your freedom; then in Argos you will work the loom for another woman and carry water from foreign rivers, much against your will but you will be forced to.'   [Homer, *Iliad* VI 454–8]

Marriage

There are not many choices for women in Homer's world. The young princess Nausicaa knows she is not expected to choose her own husband and will not allow Odysseus to enter the city beside her:

'Some low fellow might meet us and say, "Who is this handsome great stranger following Nausicaa? Where did she find him? He's going to be her husband, I suppose. Either she's rescued some shipwrecked foreigner from far away, for there's no people nearby, or some longed-for god has come down from heaven in answer to her prayers. . . ." That's how they will talk and I would be disgraced. And I too would blame a girl who did such a thing and, against the wishes of her dear father and mother while they were still alive, associated with men before she was officially married.' [Homer, *Odyssey* VI 275–81, 85–8]

But all freeborn girls would be married. Marriages between leading families were important to small independent states for the alliances they brought. The father might make the choice of husband (Nausicaa's father did in the event offer her to Odysseus) or suitors might woo a king's daughter with splendid gifts, always an important feature of Homeric society. It was not uncommon for the choice to be made by contest; Penelope's proposal was only unusual in coming from her rather than from her father:

'But come then, wooers, since marriage with me is the prize. I will set the great bow of godlike Odysseus before you. Whoever strings the bow most easily and shoots through all twelve axes, with him will I go, leaving this my married home.' [Homer, *Odyssey* XXI 73–7]

Circe leaves her loom to give Odysseus a magic potion

7

Noble ladies

Penelope, with face veiled, watched the suitors feasting; and Andromache moves freely about Troy. This suggests that women were not as segregated as in later times, but their place was still firmly in the home to rear children, prepare food, spin and weave. Life was simple even for royal women: Nausicaa took the family washing to the river, Nestor's queen prepared his bed and bedding, and his daughter bathed his guests.

The chief task of women of all ranks was spinning and weaving; beautiful clothes were very important and were regularly presented as gifts. Odysseus' men found even the goddess Circe weaving 'the fine-woven, beautiful, glorious work such as goddesses make', and for three years Penelope raised no suspicion among the suitors when she claimed she had to finish her weaving.

Some women do seem to have enjoyed particular status and respect. One such is Odysseus' mother, Anticleia, who was highly regarded as a mistress by her slaves. Another is Queen Arete, who had considerable power in Phaeacia, as Nausicaa tells Odysseus:

'But when you have got inside the house and court, go quickly through the great hall until you get to my mother. She sits beside the hearth in the light of the fire spinning purple-dyed wool, a wonder to behold, and leaning against a pillar; behind her sit her maids. My father's throne is close beside her, where he sits and drinks his wine like a god. Pass by him and grasp my mother's knees; ... if she feels kindly towards you then you have a hope of seeing your friends and reaching your native land and your well-built house again.'   [Homer, *Odyssey* VI 303–15]

Women weaving and weighing wool

Helen was another exceptional woman; even after ten years of war the Trojan elders could say they did not blame 'the Greeks and Trojans suffering the pain of war for such a woman'. She was accepted as Paris' wife in Troy and could walk freely about the city, treated with respect. Back home again in Sparta she enjoyed a status similar to that of Arete, and sat beside Menelaus, with her wonderful silver workbox on wheels, and took part on equal terms in the interview with Telemachus.

Besides the noble ladies, there is little detail of free women's lives. Some must have earned their living, as an evenly poised battle is compared to

the scales an honest working woman balances, levelling the wool and the weights on each side to win a meagre wage for her children.

[Homer, *Iliad* XII 433–5]

Other brief comments in the *Iliad* allude to women quarrelling in the street, defending the walls of a town or preparing meals for harvesters, and to young girls dancing at a festival, all of which suggest that women were not entirely housebound.

Slaves and concubines

Masters could take their sexual pleasure with their slave-women and it was normal for kings and warriors to have concubines (bed-mates), so that even Helen, who had a daughter but no son, had to accept Menelaus' son by a slave as his heir. The quarrel between

9

Agamemnon and Achilles with which the *Iliad* starts was over the possession of a concubine, Briseis; and all the Greek heroes had women in their tents to attend to their needs. Often these women were nobly-born captives in war or were awarded as prizes in contests. In some cases they loved and were loved like wives; Homer tells us how Agamemnon felt about his concubine:

I prefer her to Clytemnestra, my wedded wife, since she is just as good as her in face and figure, and in brains and handiwork.

[Homer, *Iliad* I 113–14]

The concubine's feelings were not recorded.

Slave-women were an important part not only of the household but of the economy, as producers of cloth. Linear B tablets list slave-women and children with their place of origin, and some scholars have suggested that capture of women was one of the motives for warfare. There were fifty slave-girls at work in Alcinous' palace, grinding corn and weaving. It took twelve women to grind the corn for the feasts for Penelope's suitors (at least one of them resented it), and twenty to fetch water. Maids also served meals, made beds, gave baths and washed bodies for burial. Noble ladies were accompanied by handmaids; Helen's are mentioned by name. In Odysseus' *oikos* the slave Eurycleia was of good birth and had a special position. She had been bought as a young woman for twenty oxen, and had been nurse to both Odysseus and Telemachus whom she addresses as equals. She was in charge of all the stores and ran the household with an authority almost superior to Penelope's:

Then the good woman Eurycleia, daughter of Ops, son of Peisenor, called to the maids: 'Come on now, some of you make haste and sweep the hall and sprinkle it, and throw purple covers on the chairs. Some others wipe all the tables with sponges and clean the wine bowls and the best two-handled cups. The rest of you go to the well for water and bring it here quickly.'   [Homer, *Odyssey* XX 147–54]

When Odysseus slaughtered Penelope's suitors, a grim fate awaited the maids who had shared their riotous living. They were made to scrub the hall clean, then taken out and executed. Yet slavery was an accepted part of life in the ancient world; and slave-women who were gained in war, although they mourned the loss of their own country as much as their loss of freedom, were expected to settle down and share the life of their mistress.

2

The Archaic Age

The heroic society that Homer describes disappeared in the centuries following the fall of Mycenae. The period from about 1000 to 800 BC is known as the Dark Age: writing went into disuse, and we know very little about this time. The information from archaeological finds and from geometric pots is limited. Stylised figures represent men as warriors and women in traditional roles, mourning or tending the dead. The spindle whorls and cooking pots found in women's graves confirm that the pattern of their life had not changed. In the next three centuries, the Archaic Age, writing was re-introduced using not Linear B but an early form of Greek script.

A woman was first and foremost under the guardianship of her *kurios*, the head of her *oikos*. This might be her father, her husband or even her son. When the basis of society changed to the *polis* (city-state), a woman's life was regulated not only by custom and the wishes of her *kurios*, but also by the constitution of the state. The form of government varied in different cities and at different times, between oligarchy, aristocracy, tyranny and democracy.

Hesiod and Semonides

To the farmer and his wife struggling to make a living in the poorer areas of Greece, the form of government of their *polis* made little difference. Hesiod, one of the earliest writers, gives us a picture of their hard life in his poem, *Works and Days*. He has been labelled a woman-hater, partly because he twice tells the story of the first woman, Pandora, made by Zeus as 'a bane to men', and partly because of the advice he gives the would-be farmer:

Don't let a sexy woman take you in with her coaxing and flattery; she's really after your barn. Whoever trusts a woman has put his trust in a deceiver.

11

Get a house first and a woman and a plough-ox, not a wife, a slave-woman who can follow the oxen.

Bring home a wife when you are the right age, not much under thirty or much over, that's the right time. The wife should be grown up for four years and marry in the fifth. Marry a virgin so that you can teach her thrifty habits, best of all marry a neighbour from close by, but look round carefully first in case your marriage is a joke to the neighbours. For there is no better prize for a man than a good wife and nothing worse than a bad one who makes things hot for even the toughest husband and makes him old before his time.   [Hesiod, *Works and Days* 373–5, 405–6, 695–705]

Another poet, Semonides, shared this idea that woman was 'the worst plague Zeus has made' and wrote a satire in which ten types of women are described, including the dirty, fat pig-woman, the untrustworthy vixen, the yapping bitch, the ignorant clod, and women like the changeable sea, like asses, like ferrets, like monkeys. The horse-woman refuses to do work normally expected of a woman:

This woman was the offspring of a splendid horse with a flowing mane. She turns away from slaves' work and trouble and would not touch a mill or pick up a sieve or throw the slops out of the house, nor sit by the stove dodging the soot. Her husband soon knows hard times. She bathes twice, sometimes three times a day, she smothers herself with perfume, always has her thick mane combed out and garlanded with flowers. Such a woman is a fine sight for others but a trial for her husband unless he is a tyrant or king.   [Semonides, 57–69]

This poem was intended to amuse, but it suggests that although women might be valued for their beauty, it was their services that were considered really important. Semonides complains that no one can spend a happy day if he has a wife – though he does commend the good housekeeper, the bee-woman:

Lucky the man who gets the bee-woman, the only blameless one. Thanks to her his life prospers; she grows old with her husband, loving and beloved, bearing him a fine, well-respected family. She is outstanding among women.   [Semonides, 84–9]

Woman following plough-ox to sow seed

12

Women in aristocratic societies

In a *polis* where power was in the hands of a group of families or a tyrant, the women of the ruling class might have been able to lead the life of Semonides' horse-woman. These noble women seem to have had more freedom of movement than the housebound women of fifth-century Athens. The poet Theognis was able to flirt with a girl of wealthy family until her parents put a stop to it:

so that she is weary of her water-jar and weeps as she carries it to the place where I put my arm round her waist and kissed her neck, while she murmured softly.   [Theognis, 264–7]

He comments that money is the first consideration in arranging a marriage:

A good man does not mind marrying the bad daughter of a bad man, if he gives lots of money, nor does a woman refuse to be the wife of a man who is bad but rich, but prefers being wealthy rather than good.
                                                      [Theognis, 185–90]

The daughter of the tyrant Peisistratus was free to marry the man she loved, as we read of them kissing when they met in the street. More frequently tyrants were anxious to form alliances by marriage with the daughters of other tyrants; Procles of Epidaurus, for example, married the daughter of the tyrant of Arcadia. Cleisthenes of Sicyon held a year-long contest to discover a worthy husband for his daughter, Agariste. She was betrothed to a member of the powerful Alcmaeonid family from Athens, after the first choice disgraced himself by dancing on the table.

Women were liable to misuse from tyrants as well; to appease the ghost of his wife, who had been improperly buried, Periander of Corinth summoned all the women to the temple of Hera:

They all came wearing their best clothes as if going to a festival. Periander had stationed armed guards and had them all stripped, free women and slave-girls alike, and their clothes collected into a pit and burnt while he prayed to his wife, Melissa.   [Herodotus, V 92]

In some states well-born women were receiving an education in this period.

Cleobulus of Lindos said one should marry off daughters as girls in age but women in understanding, showing that girls should be educated too.   [Diogenes Laertes, I 89]

His own daughter, Cleobuline, was well educated and admired for writing riddles in verse.

13

The most famous of the educated ladies of the Archaic Age was Sappho, the leading figure of a group of women writing poetry in Lesbos, where women seem to have been more independent-minded. Alcaeus called her 'violet-haired, pure, sweetly-smiling Sappho' – a tribute from one poet to another. Her poetry stands comparison with that of male poets of her time, but she has a voice of her own:

Hesperus, the evening star bringing back all that the shining dawn dispersed, you bring back the sheep, you bring back the goat, you bring back the child to its mother. [Sappho, 104]

Spartan women

Sparta claimed that it was given its code of laws by Lycurgus in the seventh century BC. It was a constitution suited to a state constantly at war; men lived a communal life always ready for military service, and boys were taken from home at the age of seven to be educated in barracks. While the women of most other states spent their life indoors engaged in household tasks on a meagre food allowance, Lycurgus thought that this was the wrong way to ensure that women produced fine children. Such work should be left to women of the *helot*, serf-like class:

Lycurgus thought that slave-women were sufficient to supply clothing. As he considered child-bearing the most important function of free women, he prescribed physical training for women no less than men. Then he instituted contests for running and physical prowess for women just as for men, as he thought that when both parents are strong, their offspring are more vigorous. [Xenophon, *The Lacedaemonians* 4]

So just as the boys were trained for war, girls were trained in music and gymnastics to make them fit and strong for the 'struggle of childbirth'. They took part in choral dance and song at festivals in simple slit-sided tunics – a fashion which some ancient critics regarded as proof of healthy-minded, pure living and others as proof of the opposite. Fragments of a *parthenaion*, a song for a girls' chorus, show that they were still feminine enough to delight in their own beauty and singing.

More tuneful than the Sirens [are we not] – for they are goddesses and we are but children ten in place of eleven – yet we sing as sweetly as a swan upon the streams of Xanthus. [Alcman, *Parthenaion* 96–101 Trans. Page]

Spartan girls, unlike Athenian girls, were not married until they were fully grown. The marriage customs were unusual and represented ancient marriage by capture. The girl was carried off and dressed in men's clothing, her hair was cut short, and she awaited her bridegroom alone in the dark. Her husband visited her in secret, continuing to dine and sleep in the communal mess until he was thirty. She did not appear in public as a wife until she was pregnant, and would not share a household with her husband for the first ten or twelve years of marriage. A more colourful story states that young men were locked up in the dark with girls of marriageable age and each married the one he caught. So important was it to produce children that it was said that a husband would lend his wife to a childless man to bear him a child. If such an arrangement was permitted, it is not surprising that the ancient Spartan, Geradas, was able to claim that there was no adultery in Sparta.

As their husbands were so often absent on campaign and their sons were brought up by the state, older Spartan women managed the household and property.

It is said Spartan women were too bold and mannish even towards their husbands, as they had complete authority over their households, and in public affairs shared in the deliberation and freedom of speech even on very important issues.   [Plutarch, *Numa and Lycurgus* III 5]

Spartan girl athlete

15

They were mannish in their patriotism, too; one mother, Damatria, killed her own son for cowardice in battle, and Plutarch gives several examples of their firm-mindedness:

A Spartan woman was burying her son, when some old woman approached and said 'Oh, what a misfortune! You poor woman!' 'Good heavens, no,' she replied, 'it's good fortune, for I bore him to die for Sparta and that's just what has happened.'   [Plutarch, *Moralia* 241.8]

Originally Spartan women could not own a *kleros*, an allotment of land, but only pass on to their children what they themselves had inherited, but by Aristotle's time women controlled a great deal of property and were criticised for their wealth and luxury.

Gortyn, in Crete, which had a similar constitution to Sparta, did allow a woman to possess property, compensated her in case of divorce as the innocent party, and was unusual in recognising the monetary value of her weaving work. The code of laws, still to be seen carved in stone in the remains of the city, defined marriage, the status of children and ownership of property for both free women and slave-women.

The Athenians were often critical of Spartan women; Aristophanes' Lysistrata mocks the muscular physique of Lampito from Sparta, and Euripides blames their education for their morals:

No Spartan girl could grow up modest even if she wanted to. They go out of the house with bare thighs and loose clothes to wrestle and run races with young men – intolerable behaviour. [Euripides, *Andromache* 595–600]

Women took no part in the Olympic Games, even as spectators, but they had a similar contest of their own. There were track events for girls and women at the Heraia, the festival of Hera. Presumably Euripides was not in favour of Athenian women competing.

3

Women in Classical Athens

The sculptor Pheidias placed a snake beside the statue of Athene and beside Aphrodite in Elis a tortoise, to indicate that virgins need guarding and that domesticity and silence are right for married women.

[Plutarch, *Isis and Osiris* 381E]

How far must we believe that Athenian girls were kept strictly at home and that wives never 'came out of their shells'? We have seen already (page 11) that a Greek woman was always under the guardianship of her *kurios*, who acted for her in legal or business affairs. She could not vote, hold office or attend the *ekklesia* (assembly), but this does not necessarily mean that she was downtrodden.

The gradual growth of democracy made Athenian citizenship very valuable, and the special role of women was to perpetuate citizen families by producing legitimate children. Only the offspring of freeborn Athenian men and women could be citizens, so the Athenians wanted to be sure that girls came to marriage as virgins and that marriages were respected. When Solon introduced his reforms in 583 BC he included regulations which he hoped would reduce men's quarrels over women. As well as limiting dowries he restricted women's outings, and extravagant mourning and festivities, all of which tended to keep women at home more. However, a woman was assured of protection because her *kurios* was obliged to use her dowry to support her. How far this protected life became a restriction which women resented it is difficult for us to assess, given our own social background in which greater equality is taken for granted.

Education

Athenian girls did not go to school like their brothers, although we know that some were taught to read and write. They received

17

practical training from their mothers to fit them for marriage at an early age. Xenophon considered it an advantage to a man to have a wife he could train to suit him:

What knowledge could she have had when I married her, Socrates, since she wasn't yet 15 when she came to me? Up till then she had lived a very sheltered life, so that she should see and hear as little as possible and ask the fewest questions. One ought to be satisfied if she came only understanding how to take wool and make a garment and having seen how the spinning work is given out to the maids.   [Xenophon, *Oeconomicus* VII 5]

The speaker adds that he was not able to instruct his wife until she was used to him, which suggests that the first few months of marriage to a husband twice her age may have been quite an ordeal for a 15-year-old.

The most well-educated and cultured women were the *hetairai*, 'companions', as the Athenians called these sophisticated prostitutes who were able to share their intellectual interests. Men's usual attitude to learned ladies is shown by Menexenus in a satirical dialogue, when Socrates claims to quote a funeral speech made by Aspasia.

Good heavens, Socrates, you make Aspasia out to be very well educated if she can compose a speech like that when she's only a woman.

[Plato, *Menexenus* 249d]

In fact the philosopher Plato had great faith in education and in his portrayal of the ideal state, *The Republic*, he proposed that girls and boys should have the same education, though separately. He thought that women were generally inferior to men, but that some women would have the qualities to belong to the governing class (the guardians) after an education that included music, mathematics and philosophy. These ideas were never put into practice, but Plato was said to have had one or two women among his students.

None of the functions of running the state belongs to women, because they are women, or to men, because they are men, but natural abilities are distributed among both sexes alike. A woman can share in all functions according to her natural abilities, just as a man can, though in all of them a woman is weaker than a man.   [Plato, *The Republic* V 455d]

Marriage and dowry

When a girl reached 15 her father would arrange her marriage, often choosing a husband from the wider family. Marriage between cousins was frequent and uncles could marry nieces. As girls had few chances to meet young men and men formed romantic attachments with beautiful youths, marriage was more of a business arrangement between the *kurioi* of two *oikoi* than a romance. Because of the age-gap, a husband might seem more like a loving master than a companion. Arranged marriages are still normal in many parts of the world and can be as successful as marriages on any other basis.

First there was the formal betrothal before witnesses at which the bride's dowry was stated:

I betroth my daughter to you for the procreation of legitimate children and I give you a dowry of 30 minae with her.   [Menander, *Dyskolos* 843]

This dowry represented the bride's share of her father's estate and was intended to support her; so, though it passed to her husband, it had to be returned in the case of divorce so that she could remarry. If a widow did not remarry, her dowry went to her children, provided they supported her. Dowries, which could be in cash or property, had to be provided for a poor girl by relations, according to their means.

Different rules applied to the marriage of daughters of men with no male heir, as the *kleros*, property of their *oikos*, went through them. Such a girl, known as an *epikleros*, did not own the property herself; it passed to her husband and then to her children. It was the duty of the next-of-kin to marry an *epikleros*. If there were rival claimants, the archon decided between them.

For we consider that the next-of-kin ought to marry this woman, that the money should belong to the *epikleros* for the time being, but when her sons reach two years past puberty, they should take possession of it.
                                          [Isaeus, Fragment (Th)25]

The laws were intended to protect the property for the benefit of the woman and her children and to ensure the continuity of the *oikos* and its religious cults, which were women's responsibility. They became very complex, sometimes requiring divorce and remarriage, or giving rise to lawsuits. A simpler solution when an *epikleros* married during her father's lifetime was for him to adopt her husband and so perpetuate his *oikos*.

The wedding day was marked with a sacrifice and a feast; the bride who had been ritually bathed and dressed rode to her new *oikos* in a torchlit procession, crowned and carrying a many-seeded fruit. There the couple knelt before the hearth and were showered with sweets and nuts. On the next day, friends might visit the bride and bring presents. As the chief aim of marriage was to produce citizen children, it had to be recognised by the husband's *phratry* or social group. The party he gave them could be cited in a dispute as evidence of a legal marriage:

When our father took this woman in marriage, he gave a marriage feast and invited three of his friends along with his relations. He also gave a marriage banquet to members of his *phratry* according to their rules.

[Isaeus, VIII 18]

Women were expected to remain chaste, but men were free to amuse themselves with prostitutes or even to keep a concubine, usually a metic, a non-citizen. By the end of the Peloponnesian War there was a shortage of men in Athens to father citizen children. The rules were therefore stretched to allow men to have legitimate children by two women, perhaps even by metics, until the citizenship law was reimposed in 403 BC.

Rape, adultery and divorce

Because Athenians were so concerned for the chastity of their women and the legitimacy of their children, they imposed tough penalties for rape and adultery. Adultery was considered more serious than rape: rape was punished by a heavy fine, whereas a husband had the right to kill a man who seduced his wife. Euphiletus, when charged with murdering his wife's lover, argued that if adulterers were not punished with death, every burglar would escape punishment by claiming to be an adulterer. Women too were punished for adultery:

For Solon forbids a woman taken in adultery to dress in her best clothes and go out to the public sacrifices, so that she does not mix with innocent women and corrupt them.   [Aeschines, *Against Timarchus* 183]

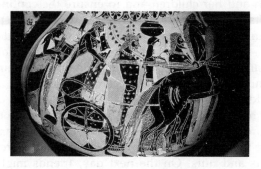

Marriage procession: taking a bride to her new home

20

A woman taken in adultery was always divorced, but divorce did not depend on proving unfaithfulness. A couple could gain a divorce by mutual consent or at the application of either the wife or the husband. The motives might include the hope of having sons from a fresh marriage or the duty of the next-of-kin to marry an *epikleros*. Normally, divorce proceedings were arranged for women by a male relative. Hipparete, the wife of Alcibiades, was unusually independent in acting for herself:

Hipparete, who was a good, devoted wife, being upset by Alcibiades' associating with *hetairai*, left his house and went to her brother. As Alcibiades did not care and took no notice, she put in a plea for divorce to the archon in person, not through others. When she appeared in order to do this as the law requires, Alcibiades came up and seized her and carried her off home through the *agora*. No one dared to stop him or rescue her. [Plutarch, *Alcibiades* VIII 3–6]

Daily life

I have a small two-storey house, gentlemen, with the women's quarters upstairs, the men's downstairs, each being about the same size. When our son was born, his mother nursed him; but to save her the risk of climbing down the stairs every time she had to look after the baby, I used to live upstairs and the women down. [Lysias, I 9–10]

City-dwelling women spent most of their time in the house. If guests were present they did not eat with their husbands in the men's rooms, and outsiders were not expected to visit the women's quarters. In one court case a man's bad character was proved thus:

He came to my house at night the worse for drink, he broke down the doors and went into the women's quarters. My sister and my nieces were

Women at home admiring a necklace

inside, who live with such propriety that they are embarrassed to be seen even by the men of the *oikos*. [Lysias, III 6]

Women with slaves did not go out shopping, which was done for them by the slaves or the men. In fact a woman could not carry out financial transactions above the value of one *medimnos* of barley, about the amount of what we might now think of as her 'housekeeping' money. Xenophon explains that the gods made women for indoor work, and his speaker tells his young bride:

It will be your duty to remain indoors and send out those of the household who work outside and supervise those who work inside. You must receive what is brought into the house and distribute what must be consumed and think ahead what reserves need to be kept and take care that what is intended for a year is not used up in a month. When wool is brought to you, you must see that clothes are made for those who need them, and that the dry corn is in a fit state for making food. One of the tasks that falls to you may seem rather thankless: you must see that all members of the household who fall ill are cared for. [Xenophon, *Oeconomicos* VII 35–6]

He adds that a wife should keep fit by actively sharing the slaves' tasks rather than sitting about. He says it will improve her looks and appetite and, significantly, make her more attractive than the slave-girls to her husband.

Many women were probably unfit and underfed as their food allowance was smaller than men's. Of the dedications found at the shrines of Asclepios, god of healing, more were made by women than by men.

Medical writings are chiefly concerned with pregnancy and allied conditions and do not sound reassuring; Hippocrates stated baldly that 'acute illnesses are fatal to pregnant women'. Hysteria in women was attributed to the womb's 'wandering' to another part of the body. Reproduction was not well understood and Aeschylus claimed that the father was the only true parent, as the mother's body only nourished the child. Classical grave-markers rarely give the cause of death but analysis of remains suggest that death in childbirth was common.

Exposure of unwanted infants was practised, though girls might sometimes be rescued to be raised as prostitutes, if we are to believe the plots of fourth-century comedy. Mothers were respected and boys remained in their care until school age and girls until marriage. As in all ages mothers worried about their sons, and Socrates quickly came to the defence when a son complained of an anxious, nagging mother:

22

You say she is hard to bear, this mother who is devoted to you and cares for you all she can when you are ill, so that you get well and so that you want for nothing. She prays the gods for every blessing on you as well and pays vows for you. [Xenephon, *Memorabilia* II 10]

Women were not all too sheltered or in awe of their husbands to take an interest in what was going on in the city, as these two passages show:

If you acquit this woman, what will you say when you go home and your wife or daughter or mother asks you 'Where have you been?' 'We were serving on a jury.' 'What was the case?' 'Against Neaira' ... (and you will explain that an alien and a prostitute had been assuming the rights of citizen women). Then they will say 'And what did you do?' You will reply 'We acquitted her.' Then these virtuous women will be really furious with you. [Demosthenes, *Against Neaira* 110–11]

LYSISTRATA Although we were miserable inside we used to ask you cheerfully, 'What did you decide in the Assembly today about making peace?' 'What's that to do with you?' my husband would reply. 'Hold your tongue!' So I did.
STRATONIKE I never did! [Aristophanes, *Lysistrata* 512–15]

Not all families were rich enough to keep their women at home. When Aristarchus complained of the burden of keeping fourteen dependent female relations, Socrates advised him to put their skill at wool-working to profitable use. This was a novel idea for a well-to-do household with slaves. Poorer women, however, worked alongside their husbands on farms and in shops or independently. Women sold garlands, produce and snacks in the market place. (Aristophanes mocks Euripides because his mother sold vegetables.) There were wet-nurses, landladies, wool-workers, at least one painter and one potter. Older women could work as midwives or professional mourners.

Women also went out to attend state religious occasions, as we shall see, and they were responsible for the family cult and the care of the family tombs, as vase paintings show. Close relatives and older women attended funerals and there was the usual contact with neighbours, particularly at the fountain house when fetching water.

The wives of the men of the *deme* chose this woman along with the wife of Diocles of Pithos to preside at the Thesmophoria and to conduct the ceremonies with her. [Isaeus, VIII 19]

So how tortoise-like were women? Plutarch said that after Pericles delivered the funeral speech over the men killed in the first year of the Peloponnesian War, the women heaped wreaths on him as if he were a victorious athlete, yet this, according to Thucydides, is what he said about them:

Your greatest glory is to be as good as your nature allows and your greatest fame is to be least talked of among men whether for good or ill.   [Thucydides, II 45]

Metics, prostitutes and slaves

The most talked-about woman in Athens at the time was probably Pericles' own mistress, Aspasia. She had come from Miletus to live in Athens as a metic, a resident alien. Like many metics she was an *hetaira*.

They say that Aspasia was highly regarded by Pericles for her political wisdom. For Socrates used to come and see her with his disciples and his friends brought their wives to listen to her although she presided over the most unrespectable establishment and trained young *hetairai*.
[Plutarch, *Pericles* XXIV 3]

Besides these well-educated *hetairai*, able to share men's intellectual interests, there were prostitutes trained to entertain at men's drinking parties with music and dancing. Many vase paintings show wild scenes of revelry which suggest why men did not expect

Women fetching water from the fountain house

24

respectable married women to attend. Unlike married women, prostitutes could amass and control large sums of money and set up their own establishments; there were also state-owned brothels staffed with slave-girls. All prostitutes were registered and taxed.

Metics and their wives who had settled permanently in Athens led married lives similar to those of citizens, according to the husbands' wealth. Most metics engaged in commerce; and in small businesses, wives worked alongside their husbands. Female slaves were employed in private households or in large- or small-scale clothmaking. Vases show them, distinguishable by their short hair, in all manner of household tasks. Slave-women who gained their freedom made dedications to Athene, and the surviving lists of their names and occupations suggest that they went on to the same kinds of work as poorer citizen women.

Religious roles

Women's greatest influence outside the home was in the state religion. The Athenian year was marked not, as now, by a weekly holy day, but by over a hundred festivals, some lasting several days. At the majority of these, women not only attended but officiated as priestesses, as well as taking part in the processions and rituals. It is probable that the Greeks thought the link between child-bearing and fertility in general made women especially suitable for the service of the gods. This respect for women's role in handing on life is perhaps the reason why worship of the goddesses Athene, Artemis and Demeter was so important in Athens.

'Hetairai' entertaining at a drinking party

The chief priestess of Athene Polias, the patron of the city, was a person of considerable authority:

For Cleomenes (King of Sparta) climbed up to the Acropolis, intending to seize it, and approached the shrine of Athene as if to pray. The priestess rose from her throne before he could enter the doors and said, 'Spartan stranger, go back! Do not enter the temple! Dorians are forbidden to go inside.' He replied 'Madam, I am an Achaean, not a Dorian,' and ignoring the warning, made his attempt and was flung out along with his Spartans. [Herodotus, V 72]

Two girls live not far from the temple of Polias, the Athenians call them *arrephoroi*. These girls live with the goddess for a set time and when the festival comes round they perform the following rites by night. They place on their heads what the priestess of Athene gives them to carry (neither the priestess nor the girls know what it is). There is an underground passage through a sacred precinct near that of Aphrodite in the Gardens. The girls go down there and leave what they are carrying and bring back something else equally well-hidden. Then these girls are dismissed and two others go into the Acropolis instead. [Pausanias, I 27.3]

The chief priestess supervised all the girls and women involved in such rites. Chosen girls washed the ancient wooden image of Athene at the Plynteria; others wove the new *peplos*, or robe, which the Parthenon frieze shows being presented at the Great Panathenaia.

Priestesses were salaried officials; an inscription records that the priestess of Athene Nike received a yearly salary of 50 drachmas and the legs and skins of the sacrificed animals. Priestesses could be appointed for life; some could be married, others lived in strict seclusion.

Girls in the Panathenaic procession

26

All the women who were chosen to take part in ceremonies seem to have treasured the honour:

When I was seven I was an *arrephoros*, then at ten I ground the corn for the sacred bread. Later wearing the saffron-coloured dress I did my bear service at Brauron. When I grew into a pretty young girl I carried the sacred basket in the procession wearing a necklace of figs.

[Aristophanes, *Lysistrata* 640–6]

Young girls known as 'little bears' served the rituals of Artemis, who had shrines on the Acropolis and at Brauron, where several statues of these children have been found.

Women were particularly devoted to the worship of Demeter and Kore (Persephone), whose story symbolised the death and rebirth of grain. Men and women, both citizen and slave, were equally free to become initiates of the Eleusinian mysteries. These secret rituals re-enacted Kore's return from the underworld and gave hope of life after death. The rites lasted several days and were conducted by a number of highly-respected priestesses.

There were other festivals of Demeter in which only women could take part, like the three days of the Thesmophoria, when freeborn women performed rites to ensure the fertility of the autumn sowing. Aristophanes' comedy gives a ridiculous picture of what he imagined went on, but we also have a Thesmophoria hymn written later in Alexandria:

Sing, maidens, and cry aloud, mothers, 'All hail, Demeter, giver of food! As the four white horses come pulling the basket, so the great goddess, who rules far and wide, will come bringing the white spring, the white summer and winter and autumn and protect us to another year. As we walk through the city barefoot and bare-headed, so shall we have our heads and feet unharmed forever. As the basket-bearers bring baskets full of gold, so may we have limitless gold.'   [Callimachus, *Hymn* VI 118–27]

Women also had their part in the great festivals of Dionysus. The wild revels of maenads, his frenzied women attendants, were a favourite subject of vase paintings, but not a part of his worship in Athens. At the Anthesteria in early spring, fourteen priestesses officiated at fourteen altars and the wife of the king archon enacted a 'holy marriage' with the god. Women presided too at the Haloa in joint honour of Demeter and Dionysus and excluded men from the banquet that followed.

Greeks thought that chastity, and especially virginity, made the rites women performed more effective in propitiating the gods. This may have given them another reason for protecting their women so closely in their daily lives.

4

Leading ladies – women in Greek drama

Greek tragedy was written by men and performed by men, yet many of its most memorable characters are women. As women were not expected to play leading roles in Athenian society, this may seem surprising.

The plots for tragedy were chiefly taken from Homer and other epics that told of Heracles, Theseus or the house of Cadmus. The poets used these stories, in which women's passions often led them to unpredictable and violent deeds, to examine all the conflicts and sufferings of human experience. They invite us to admire the self-sacrifice of some women, and to pity the sufferings or shudder at the bloodthirsty vengeance of others. The poets were well aware of Aphrodite's – and so women's – power over men; Helen is repeatedly blamed for the far-reaching destruction her beauty caused. However, we are shown women, and goddesses, who deserve praise for their goodness, as well as those worthy of condemnation for their heartlessness or cruelty.

Women to admire

In some plays, women appear as heroines boldly taking action themselves, not through men. This is often for the sake of their family, frequently their brothers, and suits women's role as guardians of the family religion. Thus Antigone declares that she would not have disobeyed Creon's ban on burying Polynices for anyone except a brother. To her, religion and family loyalty are one and outweigh her duty to Creon, either as her *kurios* or as head of state. Modern audiences admire Antigone's stand; it cannot be certain that Athenians did.

CREON   Did you dare to disobey these commands?

ANTIGONE Yes. Zeus did nor utter them, nor Justice that dwells with the gods below. I did not think your edict, being mortal, was strong enough to overrule the unwritten, everlasting laws of the gods. They are not for today or yesterday but for ever and no one knows where they originated. I am not going to be punished for wronging the gods through fear of a man. I knew I would die, of course, even without your decree. If I die soon, good! How can death be anything but good for someone living in misery like me? To suffer this fate will be no pain, but if I let my brother's body lie unburied, that I could not bear.   [Sophocles, *Antigone* 450–67]

In *Iphigeneia in Tauris*, Orestes, about to be sacrificed to Artemis according to the barbaric Taurian custom, regrets that his sister will not be there to bury him. In fact the priestess turns out to be his sister, Iphigeneia; she takes the initiative and uses her intelligence to plan their escape. Similarly, in *Helen*, Euripides' variation of the Trojan story, Helen uses her wits to save herself and her husband from the king of Egypt. Athene was goddess of reason and intelligence, which were thought in general to belong only to men. However, in *Iphigeneia in Tauris* she appears at the end to ensure that the brother and sister do escape; intelligence in women is

Woman with offerings at a tomb

29

acceptable if it is used for the good of men. In *The Eumenides*, Athene uses her own wits to acquit Orestes of murdering Clytemnestra to avenge Agamemnon, arguing that it is more evil for a woman to murder her husband than for a son to kill his mother.

Women to fear

What of the women who use their intelligence to destroy? In *Agamemnon*, Clytemnestra is criticised for having the mind of a man; her hatred for Agamemnon has led her to take over a man's role and rule Argos in his absence. She dominates her lover, Aegisthus, and glories in murdering her husband. In *Hecabe*, suffering drives the aged queen to take the punishment of her son's murderer into her own hands and she blinds Polymnestor and murders his little sons.

Aphrodite, in *Hippolytus*, declares her intention of punishing Hippolytus for ignoring her and unscrupulously uses Phaedra as her tool. Phaedra becomes besotted with her stepson Hippolytus, and when rejected leaves a suicide note accusing him of rape. His father Theseus, taken in by the note, curses him and brings about his death, leaving the audience to wonder whether it is the woman or the goddess who is to blame.

Euripides' *Medea* shows us a woman so ruled by her passions that love has been turned to hatred. Intelligent – and therefore, she claims, mistrusted – she plans a terrible revenge on her husband, Jason, when he takes a new wife. She deceives Jason by apparent friendly submission and succeeds in murdering his new bride with the gift of a poisoned robe. As a final blow against her husband, she kills their sons, despite her love for them. Yet the poet gives her a speech that shows real insight into what many women must have felt about their position:

Of all creatures that have life and thought, we women are the most wretched! First we must buy a husband with a vast dowry and then, an even worse wrong, accept him as the master of our body. Then there is the most important question, whether we get a good husband or a bad one. For divorce is not respectable for women and to renounce one's husband impossible. When you arrive among new ways and laws you need to be a magician to learn how to get on with your partner; you can't learn at home. If we manage this well and our husband lives with us without chafing at the yoke, our life is enviable. If not, it's better to die. When a man is tired of his family's company, he can go out and seek relief elsewhere. But we women have only one person to look to. They say that we live a danger-free life at home, while they go out to war. How stupid! I'd rather stand in the front line three times than bear a child once.

[Euripides, *Medea* 230–51]

In view of the dangers of childbirth (see Chapter 3), this opinion is not as unreasonable as it might seem now.

Victims and sacrifices

Euripides also understands that when tragedy strikes, it is women who suffer. His play *Trojan Women* shows how often wars that men say are fought for their women and children end in misery for them, and women like Andromache are left to judge men's actions. In several of his plays, women even query the accepted idea that having children is a blessing, if they are only to lose them in war. His choruses frequently express the misfortunes of women, whether caused by love, by loss of their sons, or by capture.

CHORUS OF CAPTIVE WOMEN   Oh my children, oh my father and my country! Everything destroyed and consumed by fire, conquered by the Argives! And I in a foreign land am called a slave.

[Euripides, *Hecabe* 475–81]

Women can also be the victims of deliberate cruelty; thus Io in *Prometheus Bound* is the victim of Zeus' lust and Hera's jealousy.

Sacrifice of Polyxena

The *Trachiniae* tells how Deianeira trustingly uses a love philtre given to her by the centaur, Nessos, to win back her husband, Heracles. It proves to be a deadly poison and in her grief and horror she commits suicide.

Suicide was considered a woman's way out; in *Oedipus Tyrannus* Sophocles has Jocasta hang herself on learning the truth. Euripides presents victims of men's heartlessness who transform their deaths into noble self-sacrifice. Polyxena is sacrificed to appease the ghost of Achilles in *Hecabe*, but dies willingly rather than live a slave. Macaria in *Children of Heracles* offers herself to save her brothers. Iphigeneia consents to be sacrificed by her father, Agamemnon, despite the trickery he has used against her and her first despair:

It all depends on me – the sailing of the fleet, the destruction of the Trojans, the prevention of barbarian attempts to carry off our women in future, when they have paid for Paris' abduction of Helen. I shall set all these things right by my death and my name will be blessed for freeing Greece.   [Euripides, *Iphigeneia in Aulis* 1379–84]

These girls are virgins, but in *Alcestis* it is a wife who consents to die in place of her husband. Alcestis is presented in a far more noble light than Admetus, who, after her death, is faced with the female lot of having to bring up the children on his own:

CHORUS   Let her know that in dying she is the noblest of all women under the sun.

MAID   Certainly. Who would deny it? What would the woman who surpassed her have to be? How could any woman show greater regard for her husband than willingness to die in his place?
[Euripides, *Alcestis* 150–5]

Three poets and Electra

For the character of even a woman or slave can be good, although a woman is an inferior being and a slave is of no account. Secondly character should be appropriate; there is courageous character, but it is not appropriate for a woman to be courageous or clever.   [Aristotle, *Poetics* 1454a 20]

Aristotle reveals his own view of women in this criticism in his book on poetry. Aeschylus, Sophocles and Euripides show their differing views in the way they present Electra in their plays about Orestes' return to avenge Agamemnon. In Aeschylus' *Choephoroe*, Electra doubts whether it is right to pray for her mother's murder. She wants justice of a sort which the gods allow.

'Grant that I may be far more chaste in mind than my mother and more righteous in deed.' [Aeschylus, *Choephoroe* 140]

She shares Orestes' desire for revenge but, unlike Clytemnestra who has usurped the man's place, leaves the killing to the man.

Sophocles' Electra feels that her grief for her father and her noble birth demand that she take a man's role. Believing the report of Orestes' death, she tries to persuade her sister, Chrysothemis, to join her:

'Now that Orestes is dead, I look to you. Surely you will not shrink from helping your sister kill Aegisthus, your father's murderer?'
[Sophocles, *Electra* 953–6]

Chrysothemis, who represents the submissive woman (like Ismene in *Antigone*), refuses. Electra's exultant cries as Orestes stabs their mother are horrifying, as though her manlike resolve had destroyed her woman's nature.

Euripides has Electra married off to a peasant but still mourning her father. When Orestes arrives, she shows the deviousness and trickery that Euripides often attributes to women in luring Clytemnestra to her death. She overcomes Orestes' hesitation to kill their mother and shares in the deed, but is then overcome with remorse:

Tears and more tears, brother. I am guilty. Blazing with anger I did this dreadful thing to the mother who bore me, her daughter.
[Euripides, *Electra* 1182–4]

This is a more human reaction, and Euripides is the poet who most often shows perception of women's position and their

Electra and Orestes murder Aegisthus

feelings about it. But he also shows the appalling deeds of women driven by extremes of passion or suffering – Agave, Hecabe or Phaedra. He gives these words to Hippolytus, who is shocked to learn that his young stepmother is in love with him:

O Zeus, why did you bring women, this treacherous curse for men, into the light of day? If you wanted to perpetuate the human race, there was no need to do it through women, but by bringing gold or iron or bronze to your temples men could have bought offspring, according to its worth. They could live in their homes without women, free. But now in bringing this first of evils to our homes we destroy their wellbeing. It is plain that woman is a great curse, for the father who begot and raised her gets her out of the house by paying a dowry to be rid of the evil. ... A curse on you! I will never have enough of hating women, not even if you say that is my continual cry, for they are continually evil.

[Euripides, *Hippolytus* 616–29, 664–6]

Revealing comments

Although the stories of tragedy are set in the past, the everyday detail belongs to fifth-century Athens. We learn that women were expected to drop their eyes before a man; that the bride's mother gave a separate feast for the women; that nurses remained devoted to their charges, grown up or not; and that young women were not expected to be about outside the house. (This last was a difficulty, as plays were always set outdoors and the reason why Electra or Antigone is outside has to be explained.) There are many almost throwaway lines spoken by men that show how men thought of women:

Man's labour supports women while they sit at home.

[Aeschylus, *Choephoroe* 921]

May I never have to share disaster or prosperity with the female sex. When she has the upper hand her insolence is unbearable, when she's frightened she is an even worse threat to the *oikos* and the city.

[Aeschylus, *Seven against Thebes* 170–3]

Woman, silence is women's best ornament! [Sophocles, *Ajax* 293]

We must not be beaten by a woman! Better if needs be to be beaten by a man; at least we would not be called inferior to women.

[Sophocles, *Antigone* 678–80]

You women have reached the point that if things are all right in bed, you think everything's all right, but if something goes wrong there, you turn against all that's best. [Euripides, *Medea* 569–72]

The majority of women are naturally scandalmongers; if they get the slightest excuse for gossip, they improve on it. Women delight in saying unpleasant things to each other. [Euripides, *Phoenissae* 198–201]

A woman can always find plenty to eke out a meal if she has to.
[Euripides, *Electra* 422]

Similarly lines put into the mouths of women indicate how men thought that women should speak and think:

As soon as I saw the girl I pitied her: her beauty has destroyed her life, and unwittingly she has sacked and enslaved her native land.
[Sophocles, *Trachiniae* 463–6]

But we must remember we were born women so we cannot fight against men. [Sophocles, *Antigone* 61–2]

For women who are wise, it is right to do everything through men.
[Euripides, *Supplices* 40]

You are strong because you have a fine son. [Euripides, *Supplices* 66]

For if you die, what shall I do, how shall I survive, a woman alone without brother, father or friend? [Euripides, *Orestes* 308–10]

Certainly when a man of the family dies he is sorely missed, but a woman is hardly missed at all. [Euripides, *Iphigeneia in Tauris* 1005–6]

When a man comes home from work he likes to find everything in the house well organised. [Euripides, *Electra* 75–6]

Sometimes women like Clytemnestra are more outspoken:

Women are fools, I don't deny it, but even so, when the husband goes elsewhere, spurning his marriage, and the wife wishes to imitate the man and find another love, then the full glare of scandal falls on us, but the men who were the cause receive no blame. [Euripides, *Electra* 1035–40]

Things are difficult for women where men are concerned; the good are confused with the bad and we are all hated. [Euripides, *Ion* 398–400]

Aristophanes

Among the improbable plots that Aristophanes devised for his comedies, we find the birds building their own state and a man flying up to heaven on a dung-beetle to rescue Peace. The idea of women debating the condemnation of a poet for slander, or taking over the government, or occupying the Acropolis and declaring a sex-strike, would have seemed equally ridiculous to an Athenian audience.

In *The Thesmophoriazusae*, Euripides has heard that the women are planning his death and sends an old kinsman to the women's festival in disguise to defend him. Instead of worshipping Demeter and Kore, the women are drinking and complaining that Euripides is giving them all a bad name:

I am sick and tired of seeing and hearing us women smeared with all kinds of filth by that greengrocer's son, Euripides. What crime is there he doesn't charge us with? Everywhere that there's a performance and a theatre full of people he slanders us, calling us adulterers, men-mad, tipplers, deceivers, gossips, no-goods and a curse to mankind.

[Aristophanes, *Thesmophoriazusae* 385–94]

None of the speakers denies the charges; they simply resent having their husbands put wise to them. Aristophanes is not out to defend women – the disguised Mnesilochus reveals far worse tricks that women play, such as hiding lovers and substituting babies – but he does make the chorus point out men's contradictory attitudes to women:

Everyone accuses the female sex of every crime under the sun, that we are a curse to men and the cause of all quarrels and strife, pain and grief and warfare. But tell me, if we really are so awful, why do you marry us and forbid us to leave the house or be caught peeking out? Why are you so very anxious to keep this curse safe and sound?

[Aristophanes, *Thesmophoriazusae* 786–91]

Aristophanes appreciates how women feel about the Peloponnesian War and perhaps hopes that a plea for peace will be heard if it comes from them. The women in *Lysistrata* so long to have peace and their husbands home that they agree to Lysistrata's plan for a sex-strike. They occupy the Acropolis, contact the enemy wives, and together use their feminine charms to make men so desperate for sex that peace is soon concluded:

We women have got together and decided to save Greece. Why should we go on waiting? If you will keep quiet, as we used to, and listen to us when we talk sense, we'll put everything right.   [Aristophanes, *Lysistrata* 525–8]

Lysistrata claims that women are more practical and can manage the state finances as they do the housekeeping; they will sort out the political mess just as they disentangle wool work. The magistrate sneers but Lysistrata makes her point.

MAGISTRATE   Isn't it ridiculous to talk about beating out wool and winding things up when you contribute nothing to the war effort?

LYSISTRATA   Nothing, you great idiot? Women contribute double. First
we bear the sons and then we send them off to be soldiers.
[Aristophanes, *Lysistrata* 587–90]

In *The Ecclesiazusae* Aristophanes goes further and has the
women, led by Praxagora, attending the *ekklesia* dressed in their
husbands' clothes and voting for women to take over the government. According to Praxagora, women still do everything 'in the
good old way', so they will put a stop to rash new ideas; women
are more intelligent, better at keeping secrets and doing business,
and they don't cheat or inform.

Then let's hand over the state to them, gentlemen, and not enquire what
they are going to do. Let's simply allow them to govern, knowing that as
mothers their first desire will be to spare our soldiers.
[Aristophanes, *Ecclesiazusae* 229–34]

The joke is that, far from going on in the same old way, the women
introduce property-sharing and the abolition of marriage; the old
and ugly get first choice of lovers.

Aristophanes' women are a cross-section: capable and eloquent
ladies, like Lysistrata and Praxagora, market women, and busy
wives, who are kept indoors by household chores rather than
convention. Aristophanes' treatment of women seems to reflect
the various attitudes of his day, derisive, respectful, sympathetic
or superior, but he adds a note of caution:

We women would prefer to stay quietly at home like good little girls, not
causing any trouble, but if you provoke us, you'll stir up a wasps' nest.
[Aristophanes, *Lysistrata* 473–5]

Aristophanes' topical plays were known as Old Comedy. By the
end of the fourth century BC, a new kind of romantic comedy came
in, with plots about young men, stern fathers and pretty girls. In
these plays women seem to have more freedom of choice and
action, as they did in the Hellenistic period which followed the
decline of Athens' power. The lives of Hellenistic women are
outside the scope of this book, but in the countries bordering the
Eastern Mediterranean from Greece to Egypt, city women were
freer and even took part in public life.

5

The Roman 'matrona' – the early Republican ideal

In the early history of Rome, the deeds of women, both noble and ignoble, were given an importance that would have amazed a fifth-century Athenian. The story of the first Roman women of all was carved on the frieze of the Basilica Aemilia in the Forum and told by Livy. It is famous as the 'Rape of the Sabine Women'.

Romulus and his settlers had no wives, so they invited the neighbouring communities to attend a great festival to Neptune in their new city. While everyone was enjoying the show, the young women were seized and carried off to become the wives of these first Romans. They were treated so well by Romulus and his men that when the Sabines finally got together an army to win them back and attacked the Romans, the women intervened in the battle crying:

If you regret being related to us, or if you are sorry you married us, turn your anger on us. We are the reason for the war and for the killing and wounding of our husbands and fathers. We would rather die than live as widows or orphans without either of you.   [Livy, I 13]

Although Livy wrote his history in the time of Augustus, he, like most Romans, looked upon the early days of the Republic as the period when the Roman character was seen at its best. The many stories of famous women he included show what part the Romans believed women ought to play in their society. The tales may be difficult to believe, but whether they are true or legendary, they do show what the Romans wanted to believe about themselves and point out to their children as models.

Such a model is the courageous Cloelia, who escaped when she and other young people were being held as hostages by the Etruscan King Porsenna, who was attacking Rome.

The women too were roused to achieve public honour since the heroism of Mucius had been rewarded. One of the hostages, Cloelia, tricked the guards and since the Etruscan camp happened to be not far from the bank of the Tiber, led the band of girls out and swam across the river amid a hail of weapons. She restored them all safe and sound to their families in Rome. [Livy, II 13]

Their sense of honour forced the Romans to return Cloelia to Porsenna, who showed his admiration for her courage by releasing her along with whichever fellow hostages she chose. Cloelia then showed the further virtue of good sense by choosing the young boys.

About a hundred years later, when Rome was at war with the Volsci, a formidable tribe of central Italy, a Roman general, Coriolanus, defected to the enemy. The story was that he was brought to his senses by his mother, Veturia, who put her love for Rome before even her love for her son. The Senate had failed to persuade Coriolanus to withdraw the Volscian army, so they begged Veturia to try. She took Coriolanus' wife, his two sons and many other women and children, and went unprotected to the Volscian camp. Incredulous, Coriolanus ran out to embrace her, but Veturia restrained him with these words:

Before I let you kiss me, I would like to know whether I have come to an enemy or a son and whether I am in your camp as a prisoner or your mother. . . . If I had never had a son, I would have been able to die a free woman in a free country. [Livy, II 40]

Coriolanus relented and the Volscian army was withdrawn.

To betray Rome was the unforgivable crime, whether for man or woman. The Tarpeian rock from which criminals were once flung to their death was named after such a traitor. Tarpeia was a girl more interested in gold and the attractive Sabine commander than her duty to Rome. When all the Romans were besieged on the Capitol during a war with the Sabines, Tarpeia bargained with the enemy to show them the rocky path up the cliff in return for gold. Instead, when they reached the top, the Sabines crushed her to death with their shields 'to give warning that no trust anywhere should ever be placed in a traitor'.

Lucretia and the ideal of chastity

Above all the Romans expected their women to be chaste. Livy tells two stories that illustrate this; they are interesting because both had important political results.

In the days when Rome was still ruled by kings, the Tarquin princes and the young nobles on campaign were competing as to who had the best wife. Fired with wine, they galloped back to Rome to find all their wives out enjoying themselves, except Lucretia. She was at home spinning with her slave-girls, and welcomed the young men and gave them supper. She was so beautiful that the next night Sextus, King Tarquin's son, returned and raped her. Next day Lucretia sent for her husband, Collatinus; her father; and his friend, Brutus. In great distress she told them what had happened and begged them to punish Sextus.

They all gave their oath in turn and tried to comfort her by blaming the one who had committed the crime, not the victim.... 'You see that he gets what he deserves,' she said. 'Although I can forgive myself the sin, I cannot let myself off the punishment. No one is going to live unchastely and use Lucretia as her example.' Then she plunged the dagger she had hidden in her clothes into her heart.   [Livy, I 58]

The Romans attributed their determination to expel the kings and establish a republic to this outrage, which made the three men swear to free Rome of kings who could treat their people so arrogantly.

In an earlier story, Livy had used the conduct of a woman the very reverse of Lucretia to illustrate the utter disregard for both humanity and morality shown by the kings. King Servius Tullius had married his two daughters to two brothers, Arruns and Tarquin. Tullia the Younger, a ferocious lady, conspired with her sister's husband to murder not only her sister but her own husband, Arruns. The murderous pair then married and set out to seize power. While Tarquin was rousing the Senate against Servius, the aged king arrived to protest. Tarquin had him flung out of the Senate House and murdered in the street. Finally, Tullia is said to have ordered her coachman to drive over her father's body as she rode home in triumph. Livy makes it plain that Tullia's behaviour made the downfall of the kings inevitable – a just punishment by the gods.

The story of Verginia shows the lengths the Romans were prepared to go to in order to protect the chastity of their women. In 449 BC Appius Claudius, one of the decemvirs then ruling Rome, attempted to carry off Verginia, a beautiful young girl whom he desired, claiming that she was his slave. Although she was already engaged to a man named Icilius, Appius had her seized in the Forum while her father was away serving in the army. The crowd protested and Icilius and her uncle were able to gain one day's grace. Her father Verginius was swiftly summoned and the next day confronted Appius, with his daughter beside him. Appius still insisted on claiming the girl, but her father, crying that he meant his daughter for marriage not prostitution, seized a knife from a butcher's stall and killed her, declaring that this was the only way she could be free. Such was the public outcry that the aristocratic decemvirs lost their power shortly after this and the regular constitution was restored.

The Romans told legends about their own men and women rather than about the gods and heroes described in Greek tales. But can these stories and the attitudes they convey be dismissed as purely legendary? Were such high standards always expected of early Roman women? It seems so. Livy records that during the Third Samnite War, when he was drawing on more reliable sources, a number of married women were brought to trial before the people for adultery. The heavy fines extracted were used to build a temple to Venus, but Venus the Obedient.

The Roman matron

Livy's stories help to build up the picture of the Roman matron, *matrona* – a word then used to denote a married woman, not, as now, an occupation. This status, as the responsible partner of her husband, seems to have been respected and valued by both sexes and recognised as contributing to the stability of the state. In Livy's account of the defeats and successes in Rome's long war with Hannibal, he punctuates his history with the reactions of the woman at Rome, their overwhelming grief, their religious devotion, their patriotic sacrifice of their gold and their joyful celebrations, as though the reactions of the women served as a barometer of the morale of the nation. There are no parallel accounts of the Athenian women in Thucydides' account of the Peloponnesian War.

A woman who had been married only once was particularly esteemed. Known as a *univira*, only such a woman could officiate at a formal marriage ceremony. State religion also recognised the special standing of matrons. After the appalling Roman losses in the battle of Cannae in 216 BC, the festival of Ceres was cancelled because there were no matrons who were not in mourning and so no one was qualified to celebrate it. In the same way the feast of Mater Matuta was confined to respectable married women.

Women from patrician and plebeian families alike appear to have valued their standing as matrons and the religious privileges that attended it. In 296 BC another Verginia, a patrician woman, was barred from the worship of *Patricia Pudicitia* (the cult of patrician respectability) because she had married a plebeian, even though her husband was a consul. Asserting her position as a *matrona* and a *univira*, Verginia made a spirited response:

She declared she was not ashamed of her husband, his position or his achievements. She crowned her proud words with a noble deed. In the Vicus Longus where she lived she partitioned off part of her house large enough for a shrine and put up an altar there. Then calling together the plebeian matrons she complained of the wrong done her by the patrician ladies. 'I dedicate this altar to *Plebeia Pudicitia*', she said, 'and I urge you to see that there is the same contest in modesty among the women of Rome as there is among the men for courage. I beg you to take care that this altar is called holier and is attended by chaster women, if possible, than the patrician altar.'   [Livy, X 23]

Women and Roman religion

The celebration of the festivals mentioned above was not the only religious duty expected of women. In the pious households of early Rome, the mother took her part in the worship of the family gods, a custom which lasted longer in the country than in the more worldly city. Early writers on agriculture had stated which rites should be performed by women, and Ovid and Horace describe them still being carried out in the time of Augustus.

If you lift your hands up to heaven at the new moon, Phidyle, you country girl, if you placate the Lares with incense and this year's grain and a greedy piglet, then your fruitful vine will not feel the South Wind's blast nor your crops the barren blight, nor your tender younglings the sickly weather of apple-bringing autumn.   [Horace, *Odes* III 23]

Women were closely associated with ensuring fertility, as we can see from the public festivals for which they were responsible. They performed rites to all the goddesses who had a strong connection with fertility and motherhood. Men were strictly excluded from many of these and became very curious about them. They liked to believe that the feast of the Bona Dea, which was always held with elaborate ritual in the house of a senior magistrate, was in fact a drunken orgy. In 62 BC, when it was held in Julius Caesar's official residence, there was a public scandal because P. Clodius allegedly gate-crashed the proceedings, disguised as a harp-girl.

A more improving story was told of the role of women in

bringing the worship of Magna Mater, Cybele, to Rome. In 204 BC, on the advice of the Delphic oracle, a black stone symbolising the goddess was brought from Asia Minor to Italy. When it was unloaded at the mouth of the Tiber, the leading matrons of Rome passed it from hand to hand all the way to her temple on the Palatine. A more colourful version of the story stresses once again the religious power of the chaste *matrona*. According to Livy, when the ship bearing the image ran aground, Claudia Quinta prayed that the ship would follow her if her chastity was beyond reproach; the ship immediately moved. A statue of Claudia was placed in the temple and twice escaped damage when the temple burned down. This was regarded as another satisfactory proof of the power of chastity.

The Romans also tried to use religion to influence behaviour. They introduced cults for women to deified ideas, such as Chastity, or to gods with new titles, as we saw in the story of Venus the Obedient. The prayers of chaste married women and virgins were regarded as particularly effective in times of national crisis or when frightening omens showed the gods were displeased. And not only prayers but contributions from their own money or jewellery might be demanded.

In 207 BC a series of portents – a rain of stones, a river of blood, temples struck by lightning and the birth of an abnormal baby – led the priests to decree a special rite to be performed by twenty-seven virgins.

While the virgins were learning the words of the hymn, specially composed by the poet Livius Andronicus, in the temple of Jupiter, the temple of Juno on the Aventine was struck by lightning. The soothsayers took this to refer to married women and said the goddess would have to be placated with a gift. The aediles issued a decree summoning all the married women from Rome and ten miles around to the Capitol. The women chose twenty-five representatives to collect money from all their dowries. This paid for a golden bowl to be made which was taken to the Aventine as a gift to Juno. There, after purifying themselves, the women offered sacrifice. [Livy, XXVII 37]

The virgins' procession could then take place, and it was not until these ceremonies were over that the consuls could set about raising fresh troops against Hannibal and Hasdrubal.

Priestesses and Vestal Virgins

In the state religion, there were a few privileged women who were actually priestesses themselves. The wife of the Flamen Dialis, the chief priest of Jupiter, automatically became the Flaminica, the priestess of Juno. In the same way the wife of the Rex Sacrorum was a priestess. Both ladies were subject to a number of superstitious restrictions. Among other taboos, the Flaminica might not comb her hair or cut her nails in June. The worship of Ceres was conducted by priestesses as no men could be admitted to the rites.

The Vestal Virgins have always been the best known of the Roman priestesses, the six guardians of the flame in the Temple of Vesta. They were sworn to chastity and lived as a community, but the idea that they were like an order of nuns is misleading. When a vacancy occurred, twenty girls were selected, aged between six and ten. They had to be free from physical defects, and the daughters of living parents who were freeborn (though daughters of freedmen became eligible under Augustus). One of the twenty was chosen by lot, and immediately passed from her father's control. The *Pontifex Maximus*, the Chief Priest, addressed her:

'I take you, Amata, as one legally qualified, as a priestess of Vesta to perform the rites which it is the law that a Vestal perform for the citizens of Rome.'

He then led her to the *Atrium Vestae*. This house, with its goldfish pools and garden lined with statues of Senior Vestals, can still be seen in the Forum.

The Vestals lived in the precinct of the goddess which anyone who wishes may enter by day, but it is not lawful for any male to remain there at night. They had to remain there for thirty years unmarried, performing the sacrifices and other rites according to the law. In the first ten years they had to learn the rites, in the second to perform them, and in the last ten

Vestal Virgin

44

years to teach others. On the completion of thirty years there was nothing to prevent those who wished from removing their robes of office and marrying. [Dionysus of Halicarnassus, II 68]

Dionysus adds that very few chose to do so, because of the tradition that such marriages were never happy. Perhaps after thirty years the Vestals had become accustomed to the deference and respect they enjoyed. They were the only women in Rome allowed to drive through Rome in a carriage with a *lictor* (an attendant) going before them and special seats were reserved for them at public spectacles. They took part in all the major ceremonies of state and banquets; in 69 BC four of the Vestals were present at the lavish banquet to celebrate Lepidus' installation as Chief Priest of Mars. Legally they were the most emancipated women in Rome, as they could not be bound by oath, and had the right to make wills and to dispose of their own property. Wills were deposited with them for safe keeping because the Vestals were thought to be so holy, and Horace used the daily ascent of a Vestal to the Capitol with the priest as an image of the continuity of Rome.

If the privileges of the Vestals were great, so were their punishments. If the fire went out, the Vestal responsible was flogged. Worse still, a Vestal found guilty of unchastity was buried alive and her lover executed. She was carried, still living, on a funeral bier followed by a silent procession of mourners through the streets of Rome to the Colline Gate. There, with faces averted, the priests ushered her into an underground room with couch, lamp and a little food. The steps were drawn up and earth piled over the entrance. Miraculous stories were told of Vestals who had proved their innocence when wrongly accused. Aemilia, charged with allowing the fire to die, threw her linen sash on the cold ashes, which promptly burst into flame. Even more remarkably Tuccia proved herself not guilty by carrying water from the River Tiber to the Forum in a sieve.

Why is it that the idea of the Vestal Virgins has captured the imagination of every generation? Today it is perhaps the horror of their punishment. To the Romans the wellbeing of Rome was closely linked to the undying fire of Vesta, tended by the Vestals whose virginity must be unquestioned. Disasters in the war against Hannibal seemed to them to make this clear:

The Senate were terrified not only by the great disasters of the war but by other prodigies and, particularly, because two Vestal Virgins, Opimia and Floronia, had been detected in immorality. One of them was buried alive near the Colline Gate according to the custom and the other committed suicide. . . . Q.Fabius Pictor was sent to Delphi to ask the oracle about the forms of prayers and rites needed to placate the anger of the gods.

[Livy, XXII 57]

Wives and mothers

As wife of the head of the family, a woman became the *materfamilias*, the mother of the household, playing her part in educating the small children and controlling the slaves. Portrait busts of women in the Republican period show women with no-nonsense hairstyles and firm expressions. The inscriptions on their tombs show the qualities that were admired most. *Bene merens*, 'well-deserving', was the conventional epithet; chaste, respectable, dutiful, frugal, obedient, old-fashioned, a good mother and grandmother – these attributes are typical. This is the epitaph of Amymone:

Here lies Amymone, the excellent and most beautiful wife of Marcus, a maker of wool, dutiful, respectable, a good housewife, chaste and a stay-at-home. [Dessau, 8402]

Not all epitaphs read like references for housekeepers and there are many records of long and affectionate partnerships, using terms like 'never bitter', 'gentle', 'devoted', and even 'thirty years without disagreement'.

Claudia who loved her husband with all her heart. She had two sons, one of whom she left alive, the other she buried. Her conversation was delightful but yet her demeanour was seemly. She looked after the home, she made wool. [Dessau, 8403]

This epitaph reveals another aspect of a *matrona*'s life, the dangers to mother and baby of childbirth. Antenatal care was limited and ignorance considerable. Even at the end of the first century AD, Pliny writes to the grandfather of his young wife, an otherwise well-educated girl:

You are so anxious that we should make you a great-grandfather that you will be all the more worried to hear of your granddaughter's miscarriage. Thanks to her youth she did not realise she was pregnant and did not take the precautions which pregnant women should and did things which should be avoided. She has paid for her mistake with a severe lesson and been very seriously ill. [Pliny, *Letters* VIII 10]

Both mothers and children were at risk, and funeral inscriptions show how many women died in their early twenties.

The mother would be helped by a midwife and gave birth in a sitting position. Traditionally, good mothers breast-fed their babies and were respected for doing so. According to Plutarch, Cato would always try to be at home when his wife was feeding their baby, and a relief of a father attentively watching his wife nursing her child shows that this was not unusual. In the later Republic wet nurses were employed more and more, so that Graxa Alexandrina was commended in her epitaph for breast-feeding her sons.

Women were respected for their part in bringing up young children in the early Republic, when even the nobler families did not hand over their children to slave nursemaids. Tacitus, looking back from the first century AD, sees this upbringing as the basis of Roman morality:

For in the old days each man's son, born of a chaste parent, was brought up not by a hired nurse but at his mother's knee. Her chief glory was looking after the home and being a slave to her children. Some relative, an elderly lady, was chosen, to whom all the children of the family were entrusted because of her upright behaviour; it was a sin to do or say anything wrong in front of her. She was in charge of their lessons and training and their playtime as well.... But now the child once born is handed over to a silly little Greek slave-girl along with some useless, good-for-nothing slave-boy. They fill the children's tender and unformed minds

Childbirth

47

with their stories and false notions and no one cares a bit what they say in front of the future master. Parents make no effort to train children in goodness or self-control. [Tacitus, *de Oratoribus* XXVIII 29]

We can imagine that women of this period, whether or not they had the support of such a widowed aunt or grandmother, had little time for activities outside the home. As well as doing the cooking and housekeeping, they had to make not only the clothes but the cloth at home. As we shall see, as Rome became wealthier and slaves more plentiful many women became less satisfied with the traditional role of matron.

The legal position – a masculine view of women

Side by side with this ideal of the *matrona* went the view that women were irrational, light-minded and not to be depended upon. This seems to have been uppermost when the legal status of women was determined. Even when telling the story of Verginia's founding the cult of *Plebeia Pudicitia* (page 42), Livy puts the dispute with the patrician ladies down to 'the anger typical of a woman'. Cato said he would not trust a woman with a secret. Nor would Papirius, even when he was a boy:

Mother nursing baby while father looks on

48

It used to be the custom of senators in Rome to take their young sons into the Senate with them. When any important business under discussion was postponed to the following day, it was voted that no one should reveal the subject of the debate before a decision had been reached. The mother of the young Papirius, who had been in the Senate with his father, asked her son what the senators had been discussing. The boy replied that it was a secret and he was not allowed to say. This made his mother all the more eager to know; the secrecy and the boy's silence provoked her curiosity and she questioned him still more insistently. Then under pressure from his mother the boy had the idea of telling a witty and amusing tale. He said the Senate had debated whether it would be better for the state if one man had two wives or one woman had two husbands. When his mother heard this, she was thrown into a panic, rushed excitedly out of the house and told all the other married women. Next day a great crowd of matrons came to the Senate. Weeping they begged that one woman might have two husbands rather than a man have two wives. The senators were amazed at the women's outrageous behaviour and wondered whatever this demand meant. The boy Papirius came forward and explained his mother's insistence and what he had told her.

[Aulus Gellius, 1 23]

Women were blamed for the Bacchanalian scandal in 186 BC when they admitted men to their worship. They were accused of encouraging the young in drunkenness and promiscuity under the cloak of the rites of Bacchus, and the guilty women were handed over to their families for execution. This case and the verdict illustrate not only the view that women were not to be relied on but also the legal position that put their very lives under the control of their fathers or husbands.

Childhood

A woman was in subjection to a man from the moment of her birth. A father could decide whether to rear his newborn children. As in Athens, exposure was an accepted form of birth-control and a law attributed to Romulus laid down that all healthy male children but only the firstborn daughter must be reared. Families frequently did rear more than one daughter but the custom of giving girls only one name, the feminine of the father's name, originated from this rule. Thus whereas a man had three names, such as Tiberius Sempronius Gracchus, his daughter was merely Sempronia. An equivalent today would be for John Smith's daughters all to be known simply as Miss Smith. When families did rear several daughters pet names, like Tulliola, or names indicating their position, such as Secunda or Tertia, were used to distinguish them at home. There was a high rate of mortality before the age of five; thus little Nymphidia's tombstone records her brief life as 1 year, 8 months, 20 days, 1 night and 4 hours. In view of this, and as Romans were fond of children, it seems likely that those families that could afford to reared all their healthy infants, male and female.

In early times, the chief aim of a girl's education was to train her for marriage, which might take place when she was as young as twelve years old. Girls did go to school (it was on her way to school that Verginia was seized by Appius – page 40); but when reading, writing and simple arithmetic had been mastered, very few continued their lessons. It was more important for a girl to learn household skills, whether she would have to perform them herself or supervise their performance by slaves. As we saw from the epitaphs, working in wool, both spinning and weaving, remained an essential part of a girl's training, and this her mother would supervise. The end of childhood was marked by the dedication of the girl's toys at the *lararium* (the shrine of the family gods) on the night before her wedding.

Marriage and property

> Gainst such a husband, maiden, do not fight,
> To oppose the man your father chooses is not right.
> Your father and your mother you must needs obey.
> Your maidenhood's not yours alone this day;
> One third's your father's, one your mother's, you
> But own one third. Pray do not fight the two
> Who with your dowry gave away their share
> To him whom son-in-law they now declare.
> [Catullus, LXII 59ff (A Marriage Hymn)]

The belief that women were weak and irrational is most apparent in the legal conditions concerning their marriage and property rights, where in early times they were entirely subject to men. As a father had complete control over his daughter, it was he who chose her husband. However, mothers expected to be consulted too. When at a male dinner party Scipio Africanus arranged the marriage of his daughter to Tiberius Gracchus, his wife was furious despite the brilliance of the match.

In the higher social classes, property and status were first considerations, but it was rare for a girl to be forced into a marriage she was really opposed to. Some kinds of marriage were not allowed; girls of senatorial families could not marry freedmen, and marriages between Roman citizens and slaves were likewise forbidden. Before the *Lex Canuleia* in 445 BC a patrician could not marry a plebeian.

Once a marriage had been arranged, the engagement ceremony (*sponsalia*) could be held even though the girl was still a child. An agreement was made between the families and the girl was given an iron ring, a custom dating from times when iron was very valuable. The marriage would follow when the girl was about fourteen years old.

'Manus' marriage

In early times there were three forms of marriage by which a father might give the *manus* (hand) of his daughter – and with it control over her – to her husband. These *manus* marriages meant that the bride gave up her right to inherit property in her own family and became part of her husband's family; she also gave up worship of her family gods and adopted those of her husband.

There were various types of *manus* marriage. *Coemptio* marriage was a pretended sale, a survival of bride purchase. The groom paid one penny to the father in the presence of five witnesses. Marriage by *usus* was established by a couple living together for one year. *Confarreatio* was the most formal kind of marriage, attended by elaborate ceremonies and considered particularly binding. Only those married by this rite were eligible for the major priesthoods.

Wall paintings as well as accounts in literature have helped reconstruct the outline of a *confarreatio* wedding. When an auspicious day had been chosen, the bride was dressed in white with an orange veil over her hair, which had to be arranged in a special style. In the presence of the *Pontifex Maximus* and the High Priest of Jupiter, as well as ten witnesses, sacrifices were offered and a ritual cake was shared by the couple. Their hands were joined by the presiding matron, *pronuba*, and the bride repeated the formula 'Where you are Gaius, I am Gaia', a declaration that she was now a member of her husband's family. The *dextrarum iunctio*, or joining of hands, indicated the mutual consent of the couple on which the validity of the marriage was based. That this was the most symbolic moment of marriage (by whatever form), is clear from the number of funeral monuments of happy couples on which it appears. A marriage contract listing the wife's dowry was then signed, and the ceremony ended with a feast and a torchlit procession to the husband's house, accompanied by songs to Hymen, god of marriage.

Free marriage

As early as the third century BC, women, and their fathers, had seen the advantages of free marriage (*sine manu*, 'without hand'), whereby the wife remained legally a member of her father's family. Her property remained her own, though controlled through her father or guardian, and she could receive her share of family inheritances.

Dowry

The dowry was the bride's contribution to the new home. It was listed in full and by *manus* marriages it became the husband's property. According to Polybius, Scipio left the huge sum of 50 talents as a dowry for each of his two daughters. The following dowry list comes from Roman Egypt and though it dates from the first century AD, it is probably fairly typical. Nomissianus begins by stating that he gives his maiden daughter to be married to Marcus Petronius Servilius.

He has pledged to him as dowry of the above-mentioned daughter an estate in the village and land in Core along with inherited land in that

'Dextrarum iunctio': a couple join hands in marriage

52

village. In gold and jewellery, an earring (very long) and necklaces to the value of 1¼ oz. In silver, 7 staters in weight. In clothing, sleeveless tunics, a Skyrian light mantle and a Skyrian cloak worth 180 drachmas. Also a little flask, a bronze Venus, a bronze flask (worth 48 drachmas), a mirror and a clothing chest, 2 oil flasks and another flask 8¼ minae in weight, 51 small boxes and an easy chair, a perfume box and a basket, the father's slave Heraida and her tunic and old mantle.

[Fontes iuris anteiustiniani III 17]

In case of divorce or widowhood there were such difficulties and complex legalities in recovering the dowry that the jurist Sulpicius Rufus wrote a book on it. The dowry would be needed, of course, if a fresh marriage were being planned.

Divorce

The Twelve Tables of Roman law had legalised divorce in 451 BC, although the Romans boasted that divorce except on grounds of childlessness was rare in the early Republic. After a *confarreatio* marriage a man could only divorce his wife with difficulty, but a woman could not divorce her husband. From other forms of marriage, divorce was easy; the husband uttered the formula 'Take your things and go', the wife surrendered her household keys, and the marriage was ended. The husband retained part of the dowry if the wife had been unfaithful, but a wife had no redress against an unfaithful husband. Children of divorced parents remained in the custody of the father.

Property and guardianship ('tutela')

Whether subject to her husband or her father, a woman could not make a will, make a contract, sell property, free a slave or bring a lawsuit except through him. If she were left a widow, a guardian (*tutor*) would be appointed, usually her brother or son, through whom she could act. In time determined women got round these restrictions by legal devices or even by appealing to the Praetor for the appointment of a less strict *tutor*.

It is clear that many women in all classes did own property and manage their own affairs. In Plautus' play, *Casina*, the wife, Cleostrata, is gossiping with her friend, Myrrhine, about her husband who has designs on a pretty slave-girl she owns.

CLEO.   He's in love with her himself.
MYRR.   Be quiet, I beg you.
CLEO.   I can say what I like here; there's only us.

MYRR. That's true. But where did you get the girl? For it's not right for a respectable woman to have her own property without her husband's knowledge. Anything she's got, she's got hold of dishonestly; either she's pinched it from her husband or acquired it from a lover. To my mind everything you own belongs to your husband.   [Plautus, *Casina* 195–202]

Despite Myrrhine's warning, Cleostrata continues with her plot to outwit her husband. Plautus' plays were adapted from Greek originals, but the characters and dialogue are distinctly Roman in tone. The encounters between Cleostrata and Lysidamus, her husband, do not suggest a woman who is under her husband's thumb: they might be taken from a modern television series!

CLEO. What low dive have you been skulking in?
LYS.   A dive? Me?
CLEO. I know more than you think.
LYS.   What do you mean? What do you know?
CLEO. That you are the most useless creature alive. Where are you going, you good-for-nothing? Where have you been? Where have you been drinking? Good heavens! You're drunk! Look at the state your clothes are in!
LYS.   God strike me dead – and you too – if a drop of wine has passed my lips.
CLEO. Go on! Do what you like. Drink! Eat your head off! Ruin us all.   [Plautus, *Casina* 243–47]

Because nearly all our sources were inspired by men, it is difficult to tell how content women were with their situation in the early Republic. The life of most women can be compared with the homebound life of early Victorian women. There are many inscriptions erected by wives to their dead husbands that profess great affection and long and happy lives together.

We have seen Catullus' wedding hymn (page 50); Plautus' parody of a marriage hymn suggests that men did not always have things their own way:

> Gently step across the threshold;
> Start your journey, new-made wife,
> Safe and sound, and let your husband
> Bow to you through married life.
>
> Let your power be all-powerful,
> Keep the man at your command.
> He the victim, you the victor,
> You must have the upper hand.

Let him clothe you, you will strip him!
Day and night while you are wed
You must study to deceive him.
Pray remember what I've said.

[Plautus, *Casina* 812–23]

6

The Late Republic – a changing scene

In the last two centuries of the Republic, women began to show a new independence and assertiveness. Valerius Maximus attributed this to one particular incident.

In 195 BC there was a proposal to repeal the Oppian Law. This law had put a strict limit on women's gold jewellery, and banned bright clothes and riding in carriages in the city. (These were austerity measures that had been brought in when the war against Hannibal was at its worst.) Livy's account of a demonstration by the women in favour of the proposed repeal shows how women who had no vote or opportunity to take part in government succeeded in making their voice heard. The debate that followed showed that the attitudes of many husbands took longer to change.

Nothing could keep the married women at home, not persuasion nor modesty nor their husbands' orders. They blocked all the roads of the city and the approaches to the Forum, petitioning the men as they came down to the Forum. They begged that now Rome was in such a healthy state and everyone's wealth was increasing by the day, women should have their luxuries restored. This crowd of women grew daily larger as they even flocked in from the country towns.

Cato the Elder spoke against the repeal, expressing the most old-fashioned view of women's place and declaring that it would be a most dangerous precedent to allow women to influence the Senate:

If each one of us, men of Rome, had firmly asserted his legal authority over his own wife, we would be having less trouble now with all the women. As it is our liberty at home has been destroyed by these headstrong women and is being crushed and trampled here in the Forum. Because we have not controlled them individually, we dread them *en masse*.

It made me blush to push my way into the Forum just now through a crowd of women. But for my respect for the dignity and modesty of certain individual ladies, to spare them from a public reprimand, I would have said: 'What kind of behaviour is this – running out in public and blocking the streets and accosting other people's husbands? Couldn't you have asked your husbands about this at home? Or are you more attractive out in the streets than at home, to other people's husbands than your own? Though even at home, respect ought to keep married women in their place and stop them troubling over what laws are passed or repealed in the Senate.' ... You can give way to women's uncontrollable and untamed nature if you like, but do not expect that they will set limits to their freedom themselves. Unless you set the limits, you will find that this is the smallest of the restrictions of law or custom that women resent. Complete liberty, or rather complete licence, is what they want. If they win this battle what will they try next? Consider the past legislation concerning women imposed to restrain their freedom and subject them to their husbands. Even though they are restricted by all that, you can hardly control them. If you allow them to wring one right after another out of you and finally become your equals, do you think you will be able to bear them? As soon as they become your equals, they will be your masters.

The tribune, L. Valerius, spoke in favour of repealing the law; he argued that women as well as men should be allowed to enjoy the benefits that peace and prosperity had brought. Although he was more sympathetic to the women, he was hardly more flattering.

They see the wives of Rome's Latin allies riding about the city dressed in gold and purple, while they go on foot, as though the Latin allies were the rulers not the Romans. It is enough to upset the feelings of men; what of women who are upset by the merest trifles? They can win no high offices, priesthood, triumphs or the distinctions and spoils of war; their elegance, jewellery and appearance are their distinctions. ... What do they do in time of national rejoicing and festivity but change into their best clothes? ... Women never shed their submissive dependence while their menfolk are alive. They hate the freedom which losing a father or son gives. ... The consul used emotive terms when he talked of a danger of a women's rebellion and secession. In fact their frail nature must put up with whatever you decide. [Livy, XXXIV 1–6]

In the end the women won their point and the Oppian Law was repealed, and Valerius Maximus commented two centuries later that this was the beginning of women's greater independence because 'they naturally took things to excess, lacking strong mental powers and being denied more serious pursuits'. Certainly they were denied any formal share in government, since they could neither vote nor hold office, but there were plenty of women who showed 'strong mental powers'.

Greater emancipation

The reasons for women's greater independence are more complex than Valerius would have us believe. The growth of the Empire, with the wealth and increased number of slaves that resulted, released women, especially women of the upper classes, from most of their household tasks. Free marriage (see page 52) had released them from the authority of their husbands to a large extent and, after the age of 25, they were only formally under the control of their guardians. Women used their greater freedom of action in a variety of ways, but the ideal of the *matrona* persisted alongside these more emancipated women.

This was a period of changing political alliances, which might affect women in two ways. Divorce and remarriage were used by husbands and fathers to reinforce new connections, with little consideration for women's feelings; Sulla had his daughter, Aemilia, divorce her husband and marry his new ally Pompey even though she was pregnant. Such marriages were not always unhappy; when Pompey later married Julia, the daughter of Caesar, in a fresh alliance, the couple were devoted.

Secondly, these political changes might suddenly endanger their husband or sons and force women into new responsibilities, decision-making and risks. At the end of the second century BC Cornelia, widow of Tiberius Sempronius Gracchus, while remaining the model of a *matrona*, was one of the first of these new emancipated women. She took full responsibility for a large household and was famed for the education and guidance of her two sons, Tiberius and Gaius Gracchus, the revolutionary tribunes. She once pleaded successfully with her sons to spare an opponent's life. This made her popular with the Romans, who publicly honoured her with a statue as the 'Mother of the Gracchi'. When both her sons were assassinated it was said:

She bore all her misfortunes with great nobility and said of the shrines where her sons were buried that they had the tombs they deserved. She spent her time at Misenum and did not change her way of life. She had many friends and being hospitable she entertained them lavishly. She had a circle of Greeks and other literary men about her and was on friendly terms with foreign kings. She was very pleasant to her visitors and used to tell them about the life of her father, Scipio Africanus. They admired her most when she spoke of her sons without tears or emotion and related their achievements and fate as though they were noble Romans of old. [Plutarch, *C. Gracchus* XIX]

The absence of husbands abroad on campaign or in the administration of the provinces meant that women had increasing responsibility for the family's affairs. When Cicero was away in Cilicia as provincial governor, his wife Terentia and her daughter, Tullia, arranged the latter's marriage to Dolabella, despite the fact that Cicero was already negotiating another match.

Republican women did not accompany their husbands on tours of duty abroad. These separations did not make it easy for women to maintain stable marriages, especially in the troubled political atmosphere of the last fifty years of the Republic, when proscriptions (the outlawing of opponents and confiscation of their property) and political necessity as well as official duties took men abroad. On their husbands' return it was not uncommon for wives to be charged with mismanagement or worse, and divorced.

As Cicero moved about in an attempt to avoid his enemies, his letters to Terentia degenerate from affectionate concern to curt instructions. Although a devoted father, Cicero was an exacting husband and shortly after this letter he divorced Terentia; unfortunately we have no letters from Terentia to give her point of view.

Greetings. I think we'll reach the Tusculum house on the 7th or the day after. See that everything's ready as there may be several people with me and I expect we'll be staying for some time. If there is no basin in the bathrooms, get one – and everything else we need for food and comfort. Goodbye.   [Cicero, *Ad Familiares* XIV 20]

We can gain an idea of what women endured in the Civil Wars from an inscription to the woman known as Turia. This lengthy tribute to her put up by her husband tells how while he was overseas before their marriage, her parents were both murdered. She saw their murderers punished, and frustrated an effort to cheat her of her inheritance. After the war they were married but in 43 BC her husband was proscribed. Turia 'showed no weakness in such a disaster'. By giving him her jewels and hiding him in the roof, she enabled him to escape. When he was granted a pardon by Octavian, Turia had to grovel to Lepidus at Rome to get it recognised. She was a remarkable woman and generously offered her husband a divorce when she proved childless, an offer he totally refused. The inscription ascribes to her all the traditional virtues of a *matrona*, including the skill of working wool, but there is in women like Turia a new independence and confidence.

Educated ladies

Perhaps the better education that was now available for girls, particularly those of good families, helped to increase their confidence. When the influence of Greek thought, literature, language and philosophy began to gain such a strong hold on the Romans, many wealthy families acquired Greek tutors for their children. This made it easier for girls to share their brothers' lessons and to learn Greek and study Greek authors. Primary schools were attended by girls as well as boys, provided their parents could afford it. A tombstone to Avita, a little girl of 10, shows her earnestly doing her lessons, while her pet dog begs her to come out to play.

Education was now valued in both wives and mothers. Quintilian advocated a high standard of education in both parents, saying how much the eloquence of the Gracchi owed to the educated style of their mother. The much-married Pompey chose another Cornelia, the accomplished daughter of Metellus Scipio, on the death of Julia:

Tombstone of Avita

60

The young woman had many charms apart from her youthfulness. For she was well versed in literature as well as the lyre and geometry and she enjoyed philosophical debates too. What's more her nature had none of the unpleasant self-assertiveness which so often spoils such learned young women. [Plutarch, *Pompey* 55.1]

A century later it had become fashionable for young women to be painted with a pen to their lips to proclaim their accomplishments. In a letter that reads rather like a school report Pliny writes with approval of his well-educated young wife, Calpurnia:

She is very intelligent and an excellent housekeeper. She is very interested in literature too; she has taken it up out of affection for me. She keeps all my books by her and is always reading them, even learning passages by heart.... If ever I give a public reading, she attends sitting hidden by a curtain and eagerly registers the applause I get. She even sings my verses, setting them to her lyre. No music master has taught her this but love, the best of teachers. [Pliny, *Letters* IV 21]

Not everyone approved of Roman girls learning music and dancing, as it was associated in many men's minds with the accomplishments of Greek courtesans. The poet Horace was critical of young girls who learnt Greek music and dancing, 'the first step to illicit affairs'.

Little writing by Roman women has survived but there were women who wrote and formed literary circles or held salons where poets read their work. The poets Catullus and Propertius both considered the learning and wit of their girlfriends an important part of their charm. In the time of Augustus, Sulpicia was a member of such a circle, which included the poet Tibullus, in whose book survive some of her outspoken poems on her love for Cerinthus.

In the first century AD the satirist Juvenal pours scorn on these educated ladies. He condemns them for monopolising conversation at dinner, comparing the merits of Homer and Virgil or lecturing like a philosopher so that no one can get a word in:

I hate a woman who is always consulting the grammar book, who observes every rule of language and style and quotes obscure verses at me like an ancient professor and corrects her friends for slips in speech. [Juvenal, VI 451–5]

Juvenal was rather hard to satisfy; he considered Cornelia, the mother of the Gracchi, too good to be bearable.

The historian Sallust had mixed feelings about educated women; he gives a lively, if biased, picture of Sempronia, one of the women involved in Catiline's conspiracy to overthrow the government in 63 BC:

This woman was blessed with good birth and beauty and had an excellent husband and children. She was well read in Greek and Latin literature and could play the lyre and dance far better than a respectable woman needs to. She had all the talents that lead to an extravagant life. The last thing she thought about was virtue and respectability; she threw her money away as recklessly as her good name. Even before the conspiracy she had broken her oath, lied her way out of debts and had even been an accomplice to murder. In fact she had sunk to the very depths through high living and lack of money. Yet she was very intelligent; she could write poetry, crack jokes and suit her talk to the occasion, and be polite, tender or bawdy. In short she had a great deal of wit and charm. [Sallust, *Catiline* 25]

A literary lady

Political roles

Is it surprising to find Sempronia involved in a political plot? Catiline was proposing to cancel all debts, which no doubt attracted her, but women of the ruling classes were much concerned in state affairs. As they had no political rights themselves, they had to use their influence with their male relatives.

According to Livy, the important law of 336 BC, which gave plebeians equal right with the patricians to hold the consulship, was in part due to a woman. He describes Fabia's resentment when she saw the honours her sister enjoyed because her patrician husband was consul, an office for which her own husband, being a plebeian, was ineligible. Her father, Fabius Ambustus, discovering her distress, pushed ahead with plans to open the consulship to plebeians. The fact that such a story, whether true or not, could be included in a history shows that Roman women had an influence unheard of in Greece.

In the liberated atmosphere of the late Republic, there were some women who were ambitious for power themselves and who set out to acquire it. Compare the story of Valeria, who married the powerful dictator Sulla in 80 BC, with that of Praecia, a far from highborn lady who exerted great influence over state affairs in the years after the death of Sulla:

In those days seats at gladiator shows were not segregated but men and women sat together. A woman of great beauty and distinguished family happened to be sitting near Sulla. She was called Valeria, the daughter of Messala, daughter of Hortensius, the orator, and she had just divorced her husband. As she passed behind Sulla she plucked a bit of thread from his cloak and went to her seat. When Sulla looked up in surprise she said 'Don't worry, Dictator, I just wanted to share a bit of your good luck.' Sulla, not at all annoyed at hearing this, was clearly attracted, for he sent secretly and asked her name and discovered all about her. From this grew exchanged glances and constant turning to gaze or smile at each other and finally there was an understanding and a marriage contract.

[Plutarch, *Sulla* XXXV]

There was a woman called Praecia notorious in Rome for her beauty and charms. In many ways she was no better than a prostitute, but by using her contacts and acquaintances to further the interests and political ambitions of her friends she got a name for being a good friend who could get things done. When she cast her spell over Cethegus, then at the peak of his fame and in control of Rome, and became his mistress, all political power passed into her hands. The state made no decision unless Cethegus supported it and Cethegus did nothing without Praecia's orders.

[Plutarch, *Lucullus* VI]

The appalling but able Fulvia gained hatred and notoriety for her masculine ruthlessness. By her third marriage she became the wife of Antony and used her determination on his behalf. When the Senate was debating whether Antony should be pronounced a public enemy, she canvassed the senators by night and demonstrated in front of the Senate House by day. In 43 BC, when Antony was in power, she had one Rufus proscribed because she wanted his villa. When his head was delivered to her, she had it fastened up in front of the house he had refused to sell. She accompanied Antony on campaign, and while he was in the East, she was the driving force in the campaign against Octavian in Italy to the extent that his soldiers scratched her name on the missiles they shot into her stronghold.

The Civil Wars meant that women also had to take unaccustomed action to defend themselves and their property. In 43 BC the Triumvirs, Antony, Lepidus and Octavian, in need of money for their expenses, commanded 1400 wealthy women whose menfolk had been proscribed to surrender most of their riches or face stiff penalties. The women first appealed to the Triumvirs' wives – Fulvia was extremely rude to them – and when that failed went to the Forum where Hortensia spoke for them all:

You have already robbed us of our fathers, sons, husbands and brothers accusing them of wronging you. If you rob us of our property as well, you will reduce us to a state unworthy of our birth, our way of life and our womanhood. If you allege that we have wronged you, as you say our husbands did, proscribe us too. But if we women have not voted you public enemies, if we have not torn down your houses, if we have not destroyed your army or led another against you, if we have not prevented you gaining offices or honours, why are we sharing the penalties when we did not share the crimes? Why should we pay taxes when we have no share in offices of state, honours, military commands or political life at all, especially when you fight over them so disastrously? . . . Let a war against the Gauls or the Parthians come and we shall be just as patriotic as our mothers. But for civil wars, I pray we may never contribute money nor help you to fight each other.   [Appian, *Civil War* 32, 33]

The Triumvirs were angry that women should speak in public and had them driven from the Forum, but they did modify their own demands.

Hortensia was using arguments that are still heard today when women are pleading for fairer political treatment. Quintilian commended Hortensia for her eloquence in his book on oratory, saying that it might be expected from the daughter of a distinguished lawyer, but she was not the only woman public speaker. Among others we hear of Afrania, who became notorious for pleading in the public courts.

In the years after the murder of Caesar, there were women whose political influence was recognised as being used for the safety and success of their husbands and sons. Servilia, the mother of M. Brutus, was the one in command of family councils on the future of Brutus and Cassius. Cutting Cicero's speechifying short on one occasion, she undertook to have the Senate's proposals for the two men changed. How she achieved this is not revealed, but from Cicero's letters it is clear that she had her finger on every development. After Brutus' death at Philippi, Antony sent her son's ashes to her in tribute to one whom Cicero described as 'the most sensible and energetic woman, who was completely absorbed in her son's interests'.

The life of pleasure

Politics did not interest all women and Rome had its smart set even in this period of political upheaval. The wealthy houses on the Palatine, the gardens on the Esquiline and the fashionable Baiae (the St. Tropez of the Roman world) were the scene of parties, love affairs and scandalous escapades. Sulla's daughter, Fausta, indulged in affairs which her husband, the Mafia-like politician, Milo, seems to have tolerated. The well-born Caecilia Metella had so many lovers that her husband finally divorced her and she went off with the rich and dissolute son of an actor.

Most notorious of all was the beautiful, intelligent Clodia, wife of Metellus Celer, the consul for 60 BC. She was the sister of P. Clodius, the reckless politician who was involved in the Bona Dea scandal. Scholars are divided as to whether she or her sister was the mistress of the poet Catullus. Her character seems to have had all the charm, wit, passion and infidelity he ascribes to Lesbia. She was furious when a later lover, the young Caelius Rufus, abandoned her; not being used to such treatment, she took her revenge by persuading an inexperienced young lawyer to bring a trumped-up charge against him. Cicero spoke in defence of Caelius and directed his attack against Clodia. She had alleged that Caelius had tried to poison her – a fine charge, said Cicero, from one suspected of poisoning her distinguished husband. Was the young man to blame, he asked,

if a woman without a husband opens her house to all comers and openly lives like a prostitute, if she has begun to attend the parties of total strangers, if she does this here in Rome, in her gardens, in the middle of crowded Baiae; if in short she behaves in such a way that not only her conduct, her style of dress and the company she keeps, her seductive glances and her outspoken words, but her embraces, her kisses, her beach parties, boating parties, dinner parties advertise her not just as a prostitute but as a particularly lewd and shameless one.   [Cicerom, *Pro Caelio* 47]

How typical were these outstanding figures, Clodia and Fulvia, or Turia and Servilia? Almost all the women discussed in this chapter had education and rank or wealth, all of which made independence easier. We shall discover more of the life of poorer women and slaves in a later chapter, but we can assume that for the majority of women life was as restricted and home-based as it

Living the life of a prostitute

had ever been. Their freedom was on a smaller scale – improved education, less control from father or husband, more say in the management of their affairs. They had to face greater responsibilities, too, as husbands were caught up in the Civil Wars and, in the country, as farms were confiscated to resettle veteran soldiers. Their motives for divorce might not have been so political as in the upper classes, but divorce was sufficiently widespread to make Augustus take steps to regulate it. Yet, despite this, there is a tombstone of this period which suggests that there were still many Roman women living in the traditional style of the *matrona*:

In life I was called Aurelia Philematium, chaste, respectable, a stranger to everything vulgar, faithful to my husband. My husband was also a freedman whom I miss so sadly, in fact he was a father and more to me. He took me under his wing when I was 7. At 40 I died, but by my continual efforts he used to flourish.   [Dessau, 7472]

7

Imperial laws and Imperial ladies

When Octavian defeated Antony and Cleopatra at the battle of Actium in 31 BC, it was not just one more Roman victory. It marked the beginning of a whole new era. Octavian returned to a Rome that had suffered a series of civil wars and upheaval for the last fifty years. He began a programme of reconstruction of every aspect of Roman life. The machinery of government was over-hauled, but though the Senate met and the magistrates were elected, all important power was in the hands of Octavian, now known by the title of Augustus. His aim was not only to restore the temples and buildings of Rome, but to revive the state religion and restore old Republican ideals.

Reforms of Augustus and his successors

Augustus set himself to remedy the falling birth rate, made worse by the war and proscriptions. By laws passed in 18 BC and AD 9, he hoped to strengthen marriage, encourage larger families, and punish adultery. These laws had far-reaching consequences for women. The *Lex Iulia* (the Julian law) defined what marriages were permitted between social classes. Marriage with ex-slaves became legal for all except the senatorial class.

To improve the birth rate, Augustus introduced a system of rewards and penalties to ensure that all men aged 25–60 and women of 20–50 were married. Childless widows were expected to remarry within twelve months and divorcées within six, though these periods were modified in AD 9. The unmarried and childless were penalised by the loss of inheritance rights. Long engage-ments were forbidden, to prevent men from evading marriage by becoming betrothed to young girls. Parents of large families were rewarded by the grant of *ius trium liberorum* (Right of Three Children). This gave the man improved status and promotion prospects but made an even greater difference to the position of his wife. Mothers who had three children, or four if they were freedwomen, gained legal independence and could administer their own affairs without need of a *tutor*. The grant also increased the amount of property they could inherit, while it restricted the husband's power to dispose of property that had come to him as a dowry. Women would be anxious to have proof that they had borne three children and they now had the right, previously restricted to fathers, to register the births of legitimate children. These measures, intended to encourage women to emulate the old-style Roman *matronae*, in fact gave them more freedom.

The *Lex Iulia de adulteriis coercendis* (adultery laws) were passed by Augustus to protect the sanctity of marriage by making adultery a punishable offence. Family councils no longer had the power to execute an adulterous woman; instead she was punished by exile (separately from her lover) or by hard labour, as well as by the loss of a third of her property and half her dowry.

A wronged wife still had no right to prosecute an adulterous husband, but her father could bring a charge if he could prove adultery. There was no room for change of heart and forgiveness; a man was bound to divorce a guilty wife. If he failed to do so, a third party could bring the charge.

Galitta, who was married to a military tribune on the point of entering public life, had disgraced her husband's standing and her own by an affair with a centurion. The husband had written of this to his commanding officer, who had reported it to the Emperor. After examining the evidence the Emperor demoted and banished the centurion. Since it takes two to make an adultery, half the charge remained unpunished, but the husband hung back out of love for his wife and was greatly blamed for his tolerance. In fact he even kept her under his roof after the crime was discovered, presumably satisfied with removing his rival. He was warned to complete the prosecution and did so reluctantly. Even so it was necessary for her to be condemned and she was punished according to the Julian law.   [Pliny, *Letters* VI 31]

It is difficult to improve personal morality by passing laws, but Tiberius and other emperors continued to try. Presumably they did not consider that the laws applied to their own conduct. Tiberius prevented the women of knights' and senators' families from registering as prostitutes to avoid the adultery laws. In fact, he used the Julian laws as a pretext for banishing high-born women during the reign of terror, when anyone of high birth or great wealth was liable to suspicion of treason.

In time, the interpretation of the law of adultery became so complex that a large body of legal writings developed to define exactly what constituted adultery and who could bring charges. All manner of situations were covered.

If a man marries his pupil contrary to the senatorial decree, this is not a true marriage and he can be accused of adultery if he was *tutor* and married a woman under 26, who was not betrothed to him by her father, or intended to be so, or so described in his will. [*Digest of Justinian* 48.5.7]

Increased severity went side by side with increased independence, but the 'official' view of women seems unchanged. In AD 21 Caecina Severus proposed in the Senate that Romans going abroad as governors should not be allowed to take their wives with them, as had become customary. This was his argument:

'A company of women ruins peacetime by their extravagance and the conduct of war by their fear and makes a Roman march more like a barbarian incursion. Not only are women weak and not up to the physical exertion but if they are given the chance, they become ferocious, ambitious and mad for power; they interfere in the army and have the centurions under their thumb. Recently a woman presided over the training of cohorts and the march-past of the legions. Think how often when men are charged with extortion most of the charges are directed against their wives. All the worst elements in the province immediately attach themselves to them and get them to put through their business. The result is two administrations and the women's orders are more determined and despotic. They have cast off the chains of the Oppian and other laws that used to bind them, and rule our homes, our public life and now the army too.'   [Tacitus, *Annals* III 33]

So much, it would seem, for Augustus' dream of the ideal *matrona*, devoted to her family and working wool. The proposal was defeated, not because the facts were denied but because 'if a woman does wrong, it is her husband's fault'. Three years later it was decreed that officials should be punished for their wives' wrongdoing, even if they had no knowledge of it.

Finally, as in modern British society, there was concern about the question of abortion. The reasons, though, were different. In early Rome the father had had the right to decide whether a pregnancy should continue. In the Empire, although there was still some disapproval, contraception and abortion were practised by women who were unwilling to bear children. A doctor in Trajan's reign advised that it was better to prevent conception taking place, and only to resort to abortion

to prevent later danger in childbirth if the uterus is small and incapable of carrying a completely developed child or if the uterus has swellings or cracks at the entrance or if some similar difficulty is involved.

[Soranus, *Gynaecologica* I 60]

He goes on to give a number of methods of contraception using herbs and medicines.

Marcus Aurelius decreed that a divorced wife could be examined by midwives and if found to be pregnant could be guarded to ensure that she did not deprive her former husband of the child. This law was intended to protect the right of men to have heirs.

In about AD 200 abortion was made a punishable crime, but exposure was not outlawed until AD 374.

Property

Despite the greater freedom granted to women to manage their affairs, the Roman concern to preserve property continued. Because she would risk losing property, a woman could not stand surety for another person. There were complex and changing regulations governing the right of a woman to inherit, from her family and from others: for example, not until the second century AD could a daughter under age inherit from her mother. Women had the right to claim if they had been disinherited unjustly. Pliny successfully pleaded the case of Attia Viriola, who was cut out of her 80-year-old father's will in favour of the young wife he had just married. On the other hand, the sons of one woman, Septicia, who disinherited them and left her property to her elderly new husband, won their case when they contested the will.

One result of this freedom to choose whom to include in their wills was that wealthy women were pestered by legacy hunters, just as wealthy men were. Pliny writes of this unattractive custom, which seems to have become part of Roman life from the first century AD. The poets Juvenal and Martial also show bitter contempt for men who get rich in this way.

When she was very ill Regulus visited Piso's wife, Verania, although he was an enemy of her husband and much disliked by her. He sat beside her bed and asked her the date and time of her birth. Then he put on a look of concentration, muttering and counting on his fingers: not a word. After keeping the poor lady in suspense, he said, 'You have reached a crisis, but you will recover. But so you can be quite sure, I'll consult a soothsayer I've often tried before.' He went straight off and made a sacrifice and told her the entrails confirmed her horoscope. Verania, gullible because she was so ill, called for her will and added a legacy for Regulus. Soon she grew worse and on her death bed she cursed this vile and treacherous wretch.

[Pliny, *Letters* X 20]

> Gemellus implores Maronilla to marry,
> Prays and pesters with presents to carry her off.
> Is she so lovely? Oh no, she's a horror!
> Then what's the attraction? Her grim graveyard cough.

[Martial, I 10]

Clearly such women were no longer subject to the control of a *tutor*. From the time of Augustus they had been able to change their *tutor* for someone more easygoing, and the Emperor Claudius finally abolished *tutela* for freeborn women altogether. Widowed mothers could and did manage property for their under-age children, but not until the end of the fourth century AD could they be appointed legal guardians to their own children. Only fifty years earlier Diocletian had dismissed a request from a mother that she might become guardian of her son as it was 'a man's task and beyond the female sex.'

Ladies of the Imperial court

Since Augustus was so concerned with morality, married life and families, it might be expected that the lives of his own womenfolk would have been beyond reproach.

There was a heated debate in the Senate about the disorderly behaviour of young men and women to explain their unwillingness to get married. The senators urged Augustus to rectify this too, with ironical reference to his many mistresses. At first he replied that the most essential decrees had already been made, but it was impossible for the rest to be controlled by law. When forced to give an answer, he said 'You ought to counsel and order your women as you want – that's what I do.' [Dio Cassius, LVI 16.2]

In this debate the Senate were scornful because the lifestyle of the court ladies was so different from Augustus' declared ideals. He did insist on a strict upbringing, however:

He brought up his daughters and granddaughters to learn spinning and weaving and forbade them to say or do anything unless it was open and fit for publication in the Imperial diaries. He prevented them from meeting strangers so strictly that he once wrote to L. Vicinius, a young man of good character and family, that he had acted improperly because he had come to call on Julia at Baiae.   [Suetonius, *Augustus* LXIV]

The behaviour of this same Julia, though, was rather less model when she grew up.

Julia

Augustus had no sons and hoped for an heir through his daughter Julia. He had arranged her marriages, first to Marcellus, his nephew; then, when he died, to his trusted minister, Agrippa, by whom she had five children. When Agrippa died, Julia was married to Tiberius, Augustus' stepson, much against both their wishes. Tiberius spent most of his time away from Rome and Julia continued to find her own amusements.

She was in her thirty-eighth year, a time of life approaching old age, if she had been sensible. But she misused the kindness good fortune showed her as well as her father's indulgence. She was fond of literature and had had a very good education, which was natural in that household. Her gentle kindness and good temper won her much popularity but those who knew her vices were amazed at such a contradiction. Augustus repeatedly suggested, part seriously, part indulgently, that she should behave less extravagantly and choose less rowdy friends.   [Macrobius, *Saturnalia* II 5]

Julia did not consider 38 as the onset of old age (she had her grey hairs removed by a slave girl). She was the leader of the smart, extravagant, pleasure-loving set, and in 2 BC the scandal broke. Julia was accused of every kind of drunken debauchery and banished to the island of Pandateria. Possibly she and her circle were engaged in political intrigue, as one of her lovers was the son of M. Antony.

High rank was no protection against the Julian laws on adultery, and yet many Imperial women continued to enjoy the dangerous game of illicit pleasures and political intrigue. Julia's daughter, also called Julia, failed to learn from the example of her mother's fate and was exiled in AD 8 on similar grounds.

Livia and Agrippina the Elder

From Augustus' time, Rome was, in effect, ruled by one man, the emperor, whatever the boast that power had been restored to the Senate and magistrates. The question of his successor became the great concern of each generation of Imperial women, driven by desire for power for themselves or for their sons or lovers.

Livia, Augustus' third wife, had no children by him and so pushed the claims of her son, Tiberius. Roman historians felt no need to be impartial; Tacitus disliked Livia and described her growing domination over the ageing Augustus, suggesting that his heirs, Julia's sons, were removed

either by untimely death or the wiles of their stepmother, Livia.... Tiberius was the only stepson surviving and everything pointed to him. He was adopted as son, Imperial colleague and joint holder of tribunician power and shown off to all the armies, not as earlier by his mother's secret machinations but at her open insistence. For she had the elderly Augustus so firmly under her thumb that he banished his last surviving grandson. [Tacitus, *Annals* I 3]

When Tiberius did become emperor, Livia was granted the title Augusta, and continued to enjoy great prestige and wealth. She had been used to wielding power so long that, according to Tacitus, she drove Tiberius into retirement at Capri by her bullying.

Livia, wife of Augustus

Tacitus also tells us that Livia was obsessed by hatred for Agrippina, whose position presented a challenge to her own. Agrippina, a daughter of Julia, was quite unlike her mother and had been the wife of the popular and successful Germanicus. Despite her growing family – she had six children who survived infancy – she used to go on campaign with him, travelling to Germany and Syria. She was a formidable commander's wife.

If Agrippina had not prevented them, some soldiers would even have gone so far as to break down the bridge over the Rhine. But that great-hearted woman performed the role of general and distributed food and medicine to any needy or wounded soldier. According to Pliny in his *History of the German War* she stood at the bridge and thanked the returning army.... Tiberius took it to heart that ... Agrippina had more power over the army than the officers and generals.   [Tacitus, *Annals* I 69]

In AD 19 Germanicus died; poisoned, according to Tacitus, by a rival general's wife, Plancina, who was a friend of Livia's. Agrippina and her children returned to Rome to be greeted by streets lined with sorrowing and affectionate people.

Nothing upset Tiberius more than the people's enthusiasm for Agrippina, since they were calling her the glory of her country, Augustus' only true descendant, the one example of the good old days, and praying the gods that her children would survive unharmed.   [Tacitus, *Annals* III 4]

Agrippina was considered a threat to the Tiberian regime and so was exiled by Tiberius' calculating minister, Sejanus. She did not live to see her last surviving son become the Emperor Caligula.

Sejanus' own ambition led him too into a fatal intrigue with Tiberius' daughter-in-law, Livilla. Suetonius' history, *The Twelve Caesars*, and Tacitus' *Annals* describe all the plots and counter-plots of these Imperial women in their greed for power.

Messalina, Agrippina the Younger and Poppaea

In the reign of Claudius the same patterns of extravagant living and ambition for power appear again. Claudius was infatuated with his young wife, the notorious Messalina. Well born and beautiful, she had borne him two children, but in AD 48 she took her reckless promiscuity too far.

As if it were not enough to be an adulteress and a prostitute (for as well as her other outrages she set up as a prostitute in the palace and compelled other high-ranking ladies to do so too) she desired to have many husbands.... She had Gaius Silius registered as her husband and celebrated the marriage lavishly and presented him with a royal residence, transferring all the most precious of Claudius' valuables there, and declared him consul. [Dio Cassius, LXI 31]

Claudius' ministers forced him to take action, and soldiers broke up a wild party in Messalina's gardens. Silius was executed. Messalina, incongruously supported by the senior Vestal Virgin, Vibidia, appealed in vain for mercy. She lacked the courage for suicide and was killed in her gardens.

Messalina's scandalous life may have been exaggerated by gossip and the shocking details of Juvenal's sixth *Satire*, but much as the historians disliked Claudius' last wife, Agrippina the Younger, the story of *her* remarkable life is not disputed. She herself wrote a history of her family which was used by Tacitus. She was the daughter of Germanicus and Agrippina and already had a son, Nero, when she married her uncle, Claudius. The Senate changed the Roman definition of incest to permit this.

From then on the state was transformed and all obeyed a woman and not one like Messalina who made a mockery of Roman affairs for her own lusts. This was a severe and almost manlike despotism. In public she was stern and often arrogant; in private she was chaste, except to achieve power. She was possessed by desire for money to aid her in gaining domination. [Tacitus, *Annals* XII 9]

She was granted Livia's title, Augusta, and exerted considerable political power, attending meetings of the Senate, hidden by a curtain. When Claudius died, reputedly from poisoned mushrooms, she made sure Nero succeeded him.

Perhaps the most famous of the Roman women who used their sexual attractions to gain power and position was Poppaea. She was rich, intelligent, well-born and outstandingly beautiful, but ambitious and unscrupulous.

While Poppaea was married to Rufrius Crispinus she was seduced by Otho, an extravagant young man and boon companion of Nero. Their adultery was soon converted into marriage. Otho, either reckless with love or purposely to rouse him, praised his wife's beauty and charm to the Emperor. ... Thus Poppaea gained access to Nero and first exerted her power by skilful flirtation, pretending that she could not resist him and was overcome by his good looks; soon, when the emperor was infatuated, she became disdainful. [Tacitus, *Annals* XIII 45–6]

Nero grew more passionately in love with Poppaea every day. She despaired of his divorcing Octavia and marrying her while his mother, Agrippina, was alive. So by continual nagging, sometimes teasing, she mocked the Emperor, calling him a mere boy, subject to the orders of others and unable to enjoy his Empire or even his freedom. Why was he putting off their marriage, she wanted to know.... These arguments along with tears and other lovers' tricks won Nero over.

[Tacitus, *Annals* XIV 1]

An elaborate plot to murder Agrippina in a faked shipwreck failed when she swam to safety, but Nero sent a party of soldiers to kill her without delay. The murder of Octavia followed and Poppaea became Nero's wife and Empress.

She had her carriage mules shod with gold and five hundred newly foaled asses milked every day so that she could bathe in their milk. She took great pains over the beauty and brilliance of her person and so, seeing in her mirror once that she was not looking her best, she prayed that she would die before she lost her looks.   [Dio Cassius, LXII 28]

Her prayer was granted; she only enjoyed her position for seven years, dying in AD 66, kicked by Nero in a fit of rage when she was pregnant.

Poppaea, wife of Nero

In the Late Empire

The excesses of Messalina and her like have given the life of the Imperial Court a popular but inaccurate image of a series of orgies and intrigues. During the second and third centuries there was a succession of Imperial women of old-fashioned morality, although still of considerable influence. Trajan's wife, Plotina, not only enjoyed the title Augusta and the right to issue coinage, but on Trajan's sudden death is thought to have engineered Hadrian's succession and to have influenced his policies. Faustina, wife of Antoninus Pius, was so honoured that she was deified on her death (her temple façade still stands in the Forum). Her daughter, another Faustina, bore twelve children to Marcus Aurelius and was accorded similar honours. Julia Domna, though a Syrian by birth, was a most powerful empress, both as wife of Septimius Severus and mother of Caracalla. An inscription on the arch of the Forum Boarium honours her as 'Mother of the Emperor, the army, Senate and country'. Her sister, Julia Maesa, with the enthusiastic support of her two daughters, claimed her grandsons – first Elegabalus, then Alexander Severus – as the true heirs of Caracalla. While Elegabalus devoted himself to every kind of outrageous extravagance, and after, when Alexander had succeeded, two women were in fact ruling the Empire.

When Alexander assumed power he had the pomp and name of Emperor, but the direction of administration and the management of government were controlled by his grandmother and mother. They tried to conduct everything with moderation and dignity.   [Herodian, VI 1]

After AD 312, when Christianity became the official religion of the Empire in the reign of Constantine, the traditional role of Roman women as faithful wives and home-makers received a new boost. As befitted the mother of a Roman emperor and an energetic Christian, Constantine's mother, Helena, used her position and immense wealth to benefit the church and the troops, and to help build Constantinople. The division of the Roman Empire into East and West dates from this time.

It seems surprising that when so many Roman women had demonstrated their ability in administration, policy-making and finance, no ordinary political rights were ever granted them. Under Elegabalus a Senate of women was set up, but as its only recorded act was to draw up a snobbish code of etiquette for women, it cannot have had a very serious intention.

8

Contrasts – working women and ladies of leisure

Roman women were always conscious of the rank of society to which they belonged and there were great contrasts between the life of the women of senatorial and equestrian class and that of poorer citizen women, freedwomen and slaves. Literary sources tell us the names and stories chiefly of upper-class women, and we rely more on reliefs, epitaphs, archaeological materials or descriptions of nameless women to learn about the great majority of Roman women.

Slave-women

The Romans, unlike the Greeks, employed more male slaves than female, but under the Empire, as slaves were increasingly home-bred (*vernae*), owners bought slave-girls with a view to breeding. Slave-men and slave-women formed unions which, although not legal marriages, were recognised as *contubernium*, or cohabiting; and often, when freed, slaves would purchase and free their partners. Numerous inscriptions refer to 'freedwoman and wife'. Varro and Columella suggest rewards for slave-women who have borne three children; the women might be freed, for example, though their children would remain slaves. Dealers might rear exposed baby girls to be sold as slaves for domestic work or prostitution. The master was free to make any attractive slave-girl his mistress; he might even free her to become his wife or, if he were of too high a class for this to be acceptable, his concubine.

The many slave-women engaged in domestic work, if in a good household, might have a better life than many poor free women. They would receive keep and clothing, and small *vernae* were sometimes educated like children of the family. Martial wrote two affectionate poems on the death of a 5-year-old slave-girl, Erotion.

Thanks to Roman water systems female slaves spent less time than Greek slaves in fetching water, and tasks were often more specialised; but they worked long hours, and holidays were limited to major festivals like the Saturnalia and August 15th, when slave-women traditionally washed their hair. In large households a slave nurse-maid or an *ornatrix* (hairdresser) or a *pedisequa* (waiting woman) felt herself superior to a kitchen maid. Nonetheless, all were subject to the whims of their mistress, according to Juvenal, if she woke in a bad temper:

The woolmaid's had it, the make-up girls are stripped and beaten, the litter bearer is accused of being late and has to pay the penalty for another's sleepiness. ... [Then there is trouble with the hairstyle.] Another maid combs out the left-side of her mistress's hair and rolls it into a curl. Her mother's elderly maid, promoted from hairpins to woolworking, attends the session. She gives her opinion first, then those of lesser age and skill, as though it were the Senate debating the mistress's reputation or life. So vital is the search for elegance.   [Juvenal, VI 475ff]

Four maids to attend to the mistress's hairstyle

One of the most responsible slave-women, and perhaps better off than the wife of a peasant farmer, was the *vilica* (housekeeper) on a *villa rustica*. Martial describes the piglets following her for her apronful of scraps, and Cato lists her duties:

She must not be too extravagant or too friendly with the neighbours nor invite them into the house. She must not go out to parties or be a gadabout. . . . She must be clean and neat; she should make the hearth clean and tidy every day before going to bed. On holy days she should put a garland on the hearth and pray to the household gods for plenty. She should have the food cooked for the overseer and slaves. She should have a lot of chickens and so eggs. [Cato, *de re rustica* CXLIII]

The *vilica* was responsible for preserving all the fruit in wine or drying it, and had to be able to grind fine flour. She presided at the celebration of the Compitalia, the holiday for farm slaves; in short she sounds much like a farmer's wife.

Slave-girls might be trained either to work in the household or to earn money for their master. The contract exists of a girl hired to a weaver for a year; she got board and lodgings and eight days off a year, but she was to return to her master's house by night whenever he wanted her to bake bread, and he received her wages.

The medical writer, Soranus, describes the sort of women suited to training as wet nurses and midwives:

Choose a wet nurse between the ages of 20 and 40, who has already given birth two or three times. She should be healthy, well-built and have good habits and a good colour. . . . She should be self-controlled, sympathetic, good-tempered, a Greek and tidy. [Soranus, *Gynaecologica* XII 19]

A midwife should be literate, quick-witted, have a good memory, love work, be respectable, strong and with no handicaps. Some say she should have long fingers with short nails. . . . The best midwives are trained in all branches of therapy. [Soranus, *Gynaecologica* I 3,4]

Freedwomen and women at work

These specialised skills, learnt while they were slaves, often enabled women to earn their freedom and support themselves as freedwomen while remaining under the *tutela* of their patron, their former master. Inscriptions tell of a wide variety of occupations, with women working as actresses, singers, painters, caretakers, nurses and even doctors and philosophers.

Sacred to the spirits of the departed and to Julia Saturnina, aged 35, an incomparable wife, an excellent doctor and a very virtuous woman.

[Dessau, 7802]

The nailmaker Cornelia Venusta, freedwoman of Lucius, built this in her lifetime for herself and her husband P. Aebutius, nailmaker and priest of Augustus.

[Dessau, 7636]

Women worked in shops and inns, often alongside their husbands, as well as in small industries such as candlemaking, lime burning, or dyeing. Some women had larger-scale interests, such as renting land or ship-building; Julia Felix hired out the baths, dining rooms and gardens of her handsome house at Pompeii.

In their work there was little difference between freedwomen and freeborn women, but it is a mistake to think of Roman women as free to follow a satisfying career: they worked to earn a living. Life in a tenement block was hard, the flats being largely without cooking and washing facilities except in the shared central court-yard, and it cannot have been easy for those who had to live on the emperors' doles or their patrons' handouts. Juvenal tells of men dragging their sick or pregnant wives round to the early morning call hoping to arouse the generosity of the patron.

Most freedwomen may have been preoccupied with the de-mands of day-to-day life, but there were some at least who took an interest in politics. Among the women whose names appear in election slogans in Pompeii were prostitutes and the girls from Asellina's inn. Moreover, there was one freedwoman, Epicharis, who took an active part in Piso's conspiracy against the Emperor Nero.

Woman bookkeeper in a butcher's shop

Statia and Petronia ask your votes for Marcus Casellius and Lucius Alfucius as aediles. [ILS, 6414]

Finally fed up with the slowness of the conspirators, Epicharis tried to stir up the naval officers at Misenum and enlist them in the conspiracy. ... She cited the Senate's loss of power and all Nero's crimes, and told them the plan to make him pay the penalty. [She was betrayed and arrested but did not reveal any names despite being tortured.] Next day when she was carried back in a chair for more torture (she was too weak to walk) she made a noose in her belt, fastened it to the chair and managed to throttle herself. By shielding virtual strangers in her agony this freedwoman set an example that outshone free men, knights and senators who betrayed their nearest and dearest without being tortured at all. [Tacitus, *Annals* XV 51 & 57]

Several freedwomen rose high in the Imperial household, even becoming the mistress or concubine of the emperor, as did Nero's Acte. One at least made her mark on history; Marcia, the concubine of the brutal Emperor Commodus, headed the plot to murder him and save Rome from his atrocities.

Prostitutes

Prostitution was an accepted fact of Roman life and large numbers of women, slave and free, worked as prostitutes. Officially recognised by registration with the aediles, they had their own style of dress – unlike *matronae*, they showed their ankles – and their own religious cult. Brothels such as Petronius describes in *Satyricon* can be seen at Pompeii; so can the bars, where waitresses often doubled as prostitutes. These were usually staffed by slaves and – to judge by the graffiti – were frequented by slaves and poorer citizens. In Rome, prostitutes were to be found in the Subura, along the walls and near the Circus Maximus.

Syria has poured into Rome ... the girls who are made to ply near the Circus. Go there, if you fancy a tart with a gaudy foreign head-dress. [Juvenal, III 65–6]

By contrast, the high-class courtesans had attractive homes and an older woman as companion. Witty, accomplished and well read, they were able to choose their lovers. They, as well as the new 'liberated ladies', are the subject of the poems of Propertius, Tibullus and Horace, and Ovid wrote the third book of *Ars Amatoria*, 'The Art of Love', to teach them how to win and keep their lovers:

Anxiously you wait for me to lead you to the parties and you seek my advice for this too. Arrive late, and enter gracefully when the lamps are lit. Delay will make your coming the more welcome; there is great allure in delay. Although you are plain, you will seem beautiful to the tipsy and darkness will disguise your blemishes.   [Ovid, *Ars Amatoria* III 749–54]

Actresses were regarded in the same light as prostitutes and even if they had retired, both were forbidden to marry citizens. M. Antony gave great offence by taking his mistress, the actress Cytheris, to public occasions.

And in the middle of the official escort was carried an actress in an open litter, a woman the decent citizens of the town were forced to meet and greet.   [Cicero, *Philippic* II 58]

Ladies of leisure

For women with time to spare, there were the public baths and free entertainments. Juvenal describes women swooning over the performers in the theatre, and circus games were so popular that women practised sword drill and a senator's wife ran off with a gladiator. In the *Ars Amatoria* Ovid suggests the chariot races in the Circus Maximus as a good place to find a girlfriend. In the *Fasti* he describes the holidays on such festivals as the Anna Perenna when, after toasting long life at country picnics on the banks of the Tiber, drunken old men and women totter home together.

The mystery religions, with their initiation ceremonies and secret rites, also offered women an escape from everyday life. Juvenal accused women of dishonouring even state cults with their excesses and said the music and dancing of the mysteries excited them to sexual orgies. There had been scandals in the worship of Bacchus and of Isis, so this may have been partly true. But despite the sexual overtones of some rituals, mystery religions, particularly Isis worship and later Christianity, did offer women, whatever their status, equal chance to take part and a hope of a better life to come.

Conflicting views of women

According to Juvenal's *Satires*, particularly the Sixth, all women were little better than prostitutes. Obsessed with money and sex, they took the Empress Messalina for their example.

Nowadays all women high and low have the same lusts.   [Juvenal, VI 349]

He catalogues their faults: they are mad for theatres, musicians and gladiators; they use witchcraft and poisons; they consult fortune-tellers. Rich wives are tyrannical and *all* wives make their husbands' lives a misery; they take degrading lovers and have abortions. They turn religious rites into orgies, ill-treat slaves, gossip and get drunk. Juvenal's constant theme is women's immorality, their unfaithfulness and extravagance.

She wears out her wedding veil swopping homes; then she ups and off to return to the marriage she despised, leaving the wedding decorations still fresh behind her. So the number grows; that makes eight husbands in five years – it ought to be carved on her tombstone.   [Juvenal, VI 225–30]

Martial tends to support this view of women who have abandoned the old ideals and are only interested in pleasure. He does not want a rich wife as 'a wife should be inferior'. Ovid speaks of women at the races and at the theatre meeting men, which suggests that, by then, women were much freer and could choose for themselves. Yet both claim that in the country Virgil's old ideal of the hardworking wife and partner persisted:

Some farmers sit up late at night and sharpen stakes; meanwhile the wife, cheering the lengthy task with a song, sends the rattling shuttle through the loom, or reduces sweet wine over the fire and takes the scum off the boiling pan with a bundle of leaves.   [Virgil, *Georgics* I 291–6]

Such women found their pleasures in country festivals and even Juvenal describes them sitting in a grassy theatre with babies in their laps.

Nor were all wealthy women selfish and extravagant; many were benefactors to their communities. Eumachia of Pompeii built a splendid guildhall; Scholastica restored the public baths at Ephesus. Both ladies had their generosity marked by imposing statues, and similar statues commemorate similar women all over the Empire.

The women Pliny writes to or about in his letters also seem to have preserved old-fashioned values: the invalid Tullus was nursed devotedly by his wife; Fannia made herself ill looking after a sick Vestal Virgin, and the widowed Corolla Hispulla worried about bringing up her son. He writes too of parents seeking to arrange good marriages for their daughters and of young girls who were models of affection, modesty and restraint. Tombstones of the period continue to mention the traditional virtues of chastity and piety. So it seems that the ideal of the *matrona* was still alive, particularly away from Rome.

Statue of Eumachia put up in Pompeii

There were new models of womanly virtue too, influenced more by Stoic philosophy than patriotism. Tacitus tells of the loyalty and resolution of wives and daughters, ready to share the exile or death of men accused by the emperors of treason. Seneca and Paulina opened their veins and would have died together had not Nero ordered Paulina to be saved. Most famous of all for her devotion to her husband was Arria, who hired a fishing boat to follow him to Rome when he was arrested for treason. Then, to avoid the disgrace of execution, she set him the example of suicide:

That was a glorious deed of hers, to draw the blade, plunge it in her heart, pull out the dagger and hand it to her husband with the immortal, almost divine words: 'Paetus, it doesn't hurt.'   [Pliny, *Letters* III 16]

Conclusion

We have seen the differences between women's lives in Sparta and Athens, and how the quiet lives of early Roman *matronae* were replaced by much more varied lifestyles in Imperial times. We can appreciate how much Penelope's world differed from Poppaea's. So when we talk of women in the ancient world, we must always bear in mind the time and place and their position in society. Broad generalisations can only ever be partly true.

In all things, save wedlock, I support the male. [Aeschylus, *Eumenides* 707]

The unmarried Maiden Athene was the most respected of the gods worshipped in Athens. By making her speak this line, Aeschylus seems to be attributing divine approval to the masculine world of his time. Despite their devotion to their goddesses, the Greeks thought human women were there to serve them, to be a legitimate prize of war, to supply their physical needs, to bear their children, to work for their prosperity, to entertain them and finally to bury them and observe the cult of the dead. Today such ideas have more in common with Eastern than Western views on women. In many Islamic countries the submissive, housebound life of Greek women would not seem strange. What surprises us is that there was so little attempt by women to change their lot, and that women who acted independently remained a tiny minority. We lack the evidence written by women to know how content they were, or how far they were able to manipulate men for their own purposes. Even in the more liberated atmosphere of the Roman Empire, women mostly fared worse than men: consider the huge numbers exploited as prostitutes. Certainly many Roman women were more assertive: whereas from the Roman world we have the names and stories of countless historical women, among the

Greeks the names that we remember are from literature. The private lives of most Greek women remain private.

Odysseus, the wife you won had every virtue, so good was the understanding of excellent Penelope, daughter of Icarius. She always remembered her wedded husband, Odysseus. The fame of her virtue will never perish, but the immortals will make men a lovely tale of prudent Penelope. [Homer, *Odyssey* XXIV 193–8]

Index

adultery
  Greece 20–1
  Rome 68–70, 73
Aeschylus 32–5
Aphrodite 4, 28, 30
aristocratic society 13
Aristophanes 23, 27, 35–7
art
  Greece 1–2
  Rome 2
Artemis 4, 27
Athene 4–5, 25–6, 29–30, 88
Augustus 68–73

chastity
  Greece 17, 20, 27
  Rome 39–41, 43
childbirth
  Greece 22
  Rome 46–7, 71, 81
comedy 35–7, 53–5
concubines
  Greece 9–10, 20
  Rome 79

daily life: Athens 21–3
Demeter 27
divorce
  Greece 20–1
  Rome 53, 68–70
dowry
  Greece 18–19
  Rome 52

education
  Greece 13, 17–18
  Rome 50, 60–2
Electra 32–5

epikleros 19
Euripides 16, 23, 29–35

festivals: Athens 25–7
freedwomen 81–2

health
  Greece 14, 22
  Rome 46
Helen 5, 9, 28–9
Hera 4
Hesiod 3, 11–12
hetairai 18, 21, 24–5
Homer 4–10, 28

Iliad 4–10

kurios 11, 17, 19, 28

leisure, life of: Rome 65–7, 84
Livia 73–5
Livy's heroines 38–43

marriage
  Greece 7, 13–15, 18–20
  Rome 50–2, 58, 68–9
matrona 41–2, 67, 70
Messalina 75–6
metics 20, 25
Minoans 3
motherhood
  Greece 22–3
  Rome 46–8, 69
Mycenae 3

Nausicaa 7–8

Odyssey 4–10

oikos 6, 11, 19

Penelope 6–10, 88–9
Plato 18
political interests: Rome 63–5, 82
Poppaea 76–7
priestesses
  Greece 25–7
  Rome 43–6
property
  Greece 15–16, 19
  Rome 53–4, 71–2
prostitutes
  Greece 24–5
  Rome 83–4

religion
  Greece 19, 25–7

Rome 42–6, 84

Sappho 14
Semonides 12
slaves
  Greece 9–10, 22, 24–5
  Rome 79–81
Sophocles 29–35
Spartan women 14–16

tragedy 28–35
tutela 53, 69, 72
tyrants 13

Vestal Virgins 44–6

weddings
  Greece 19–20
  Rome 51